Hunting Season

D1300816

Hunting Season

A Field Guide to Targeting and Capturing the Perfect Man

Elle

AVON

An Imprint of HarperCollinsPublishers

FIRST AVON PAPERBACK EDITION PUBLISHED 2010.

Designed by Diahann Sturge

Library of Congress Cataloging-in-Publication Data
  Elle.
    Hunting season : a field guide to targeting and capturing the perfect man /
  Elle.—1st ed.
      p. cm.
    ISBN 978-0-06-178029-5
    1. Mate selection—United States. 2. Dating (Social customs)—United
  States. 3. Men—United States—Psychology. I. Elle. II. Title.
  HQ801.H948 2010
  646.7'70820973—dc22

10 11 12 13 14 OV/RRD 10 9 8 7 6 5 4 3 2 1

For my father, who was a perfect man
For my mother, who taught me about men
For my sister, who married a great man
and for my son, who grew into a wonderful man

Contents

Acknowledgments

I would like to express my gratitude to some of the people
who have helped me along the way:

Mr. Garcia, for seeing the value in my ideas and
starting me on my journey.

Alexandra Machinist, agent extraordinaire.
Without her guidance and knowledge this book
would have never materialized.

The unsung genii of the Avon Books staff, especially my editor,
Katherine Nintzel, whose talents allowed me to produce
a work I can be proud of.

My friends Gray and Ben Henderson for giving me
friendship and hunting tips;
Granola Nancy for guidance on the process
of writing and thinking;
Lisa for being a big fan; and the whole Fine family
for laughing the loudest.

My family as a whole, especially my son,
who went without my attention while I was trying to "get" creative.

The many men in my life.
Without their honesty I could not have perfected the hunt.

My favorite authors and the characters they have
provided me for those lonely months:
Diana Gabaldon and Jamie, Clive Cussler and Dirk,
C. S. Forester and Horatio, and
Alexander Dumas and all the musketeers
(I do love a man in uniform).

The US Marine Corps, for the men of honor they turn out.
Semper Fi.

Michael, Pedro, Fadzio, Cara, #78,
and the Five Towns Community as a whole.

And a special and final thank you to HP,
for walking with me when I couldn't walk alone.

Hunting Season

Chapter 1

Open Season

*T*allyho! The Hunt is afoot, love is in the air and, ladies, so should be your heels. April 1, All Fools' Day, marks the official opening of **Hunting Season.** And it's the perfect day to begin hunting—but let's not get ahead of ourselves. I know you're asking, "What season and why is there a season?" As with any good hunt, we need to start from the beginning.

Open Season on men begins on April 1 and ends on September 30. This occurs every year, without exception. Outside of this time frame, I do not hunt men and neither should you. I know that to your untrained ears that sounds a bit strict. But, trust me, there are very good reasons for this.

It's quite simple: Most animals are hunted during a specific season, and **hunters** are regulated to make sure that they hunt only during that period. This is so the prey is not depleted during the time that they are procreating. Since we are not actually killing our prey, we want to hunt during the time nature turns all men into procreating animals. That doesn't necessarily mean we want to make a baby on the first date. But it's a time when men's hormones, like those of all animals, are most aggressive, making them perfect for the plucking or fucking.

You have always heard how spring turns a man's fancy? Well, ladies, that fancy is just what we are after! So we must take advantage of that "turn." (We will discuss in Chapter 7 what happens when you **poach**, or hunt outside the **Open Season**.)

Open Season is a time of year when fun, sun and the sexual energy of nature is swirling around us. But there is another reason why these months are the **Open Season**: the absence of **Tension Days**. **Tension Days**, simply defined, are those days that require either family interactions and introductions or the anticipation of **love tokens**. Women somehow always think that **Tension Days** are good for a budding relationship. But, mark my words, they are surefire romance killers.

Here's a list of those days: Thanksgiving, Christmas, Chanukah, New Year's Eve, Super Bowl Sunday, Valentine's Day and St. Patrick's Day. The last four are the worst. Be honest now: how many of your breakups have occurred in or around one of these days? How many fights have you had with past lovers regarding the Super Bowl or Valentine's Day? You know exactly what I'm talking about. Any woman over twenty-three has had at least one of these **Tension Day** fights or breakups. It's inevitable, and it's often our fault. We are always looking for the man to act in a certain way or give us a certain gift—often something "shiny"—and, no matter what, he always falls short. Whether it's how your family perceived him, how he chewed with his mouth open, how he declared Christmas a non-religious holiday, how he came home drunk from a Super Bowl party or, worst of all, how he stated that he'd like to get "a piece of that," referring to the Coors Light girls, the man is always in the wrong on **Tension Days**.

An Elle Real-Life Example: **Tension Day** Disaster

Once, way back when I was entrenched in a relationship, Christmas came around. Christmas is also my birthday, and I thought, "Here it comes, baby! The granddaddy of all presents: *the ring*." I went out and got a French manicure. I found the perfect outfit. I did extra Kegel exercises to ensure that the thank-you-I-will-marry-you sex would be good and tight.

We went to our favorite restaurant, where I proceeded to inhale my dinner and gulp my wine so that we could get to dessert (the natural moment for him to propose, of course). And sure enough, he reached into his jacket pocket and with a smile pulled out a little black velvet box. My excitement grew as he slid it carefully across the white linen tablecloth. Time seemed to stand still. I couldn't wait for it to reach my side. Finally I exhaled, reached across the table, and grabbed for it with the greatest of anticipation

Ooooohhhh, was it pretty. But there was one problem. It was a large pearl surrounded by diamonds. *A pearl,* I thought. *Okay. It's not the shine I was expecting, but I can work with it.*

I can have it reset later with a diamond. The important thing is that I got the ring. Now where's the question?

Bad news, ladies. The question would not be found at that table. He told me it was too soon and I was too young. *Too young?* I thought. If I wasn't too young for him to bed me down, I sure as hell wasn't too young for The Question! Furious doesn't even begin to describe my rage. I took the ring, slipped it on and gave him a half-assed smile that matched his half-assed proposal. I figured that while I thought about what I wanted to do, I might as well wear the ring. Any ring was better than nothing, and besides, I deserved something for putting up with his mother and family for so long.

To make a long story short, I went to college and met another **buck,** and when that one did finally ask The Question, I broke out into a cold sweat and explained to him that I was . . . too young. Too young and too excited about the world of **bucks** that I had discovered in college. This is really when I realized that I was not and never would be a one-**buck hunter**. The hunt itself is too much fun for me to just settle for one "prize." I wanted (and still want) a whole collection.

So, **Tension Days** all occur during the **Off Season**. The only holiday that you will have to face during **Open Season** is Mother's Day. Given that this is such a personal day (and hopefully, your **buck**'s mother is still living), he will most likely spend Mother's Day with his family and you with yours, eliminating the risk of danger. Certainly, there are a few exceptions: if his mother is a complete psycho, for example, and he doesn't speak to her; or if she is no longer with the living. Actually, if your **buck's** mother has, unfortunately, passed (not that I wish that on him), you have a potential silver lining: there is a greater likelihood that he will be very kind and caring to your mom, which will rack up some useful brownie points for him.

All in all, Mother's Day doesn't really pose a problem, as long as you are appropriately cautious. And that's the only day in **Open Season** you have to think about. The rest of the season is filled with fun, beach holidays, skin-showing outfits and warm breezes: the perfect storm for **hunting**.

We **hunters** have six months to go into the wild, find our prey and bring it home. There are two **capture methods** available to a **hunter: Bag 'n' Tag** and **Trophy Hunting**. In later chapters we will discuss these methods in detail, but for now, girls, I just want you to take note of one very important hunting rule: you need to decide upon one method and stick to it for the duration of the season. You cannot **method jump** intra-season. If you decide to change your capture method, you must do so during **Off Season,** so that you can properly prepare for **Open Season**. (**Off Season** is when you get all your **hunting gear** ready and set up your **deer stand**. A productive **Off Season** leads to a fruitful **Open Season**.)

An Introduction to the Hunting Methods

Here's the quick version of the two methods (again, we'll discuss them in more detail in Chapters 4 and 5). When you choose to **Bag 'n' Tag,** you're looking to capture a **buck** for anything from one hour to one week, and **tag** him for future fun. There is no commitment from either party other than committing to enjoying the time you spend together. **Trophy Hunting** is the final hunt. When you **Trophy Hunt** you are looking for that **buck** you want to **mount**, to screw to your **wall** (forgive the pun) forever as your life partner.

The best **hunters** can achieve either method. I'm usually a **Bag 'n' Tagger**, but I did once successfully **Trophy Hunt**.

Years ago I tracked down the perfect **buck** and nailed him to my wall. Then I realized he didn't go with my décor, so out he went. But that's me. You, the **hunter**, must decide which method is right for you so that you can then hunt accordingly. You have all of **Off Season** to think about what will be right for you in the coming months, so that when **Open Season** rolls around, you are ready to move forward.

Caution: Open Season Does Not Mean "Go Crazy"

I can always tell when **Open Season** is about to begin. By the opening day, almost anyone makes me salivate. All **hunters** must beware: watch out for that first week. Though it's tempting to rush into hunting after a long **Off Season**, take it slow and get into the groove. As you start to visit the **deer stands** you have cultivated and pass through your **kill zones**, you may get a bit over-eager. Slow down. Hunting takes as much patience as it does skill. Believe it or not, you have time. Don't let the "biological clock" or outside pressures cause you to put the pedal to the metal.

I have this friend, let's call her Ms. Gung-Ho. She had a goal: she wanted a child and husband. But, rather than take her time and hunt consciously, she jumped on the first **buck** who asked her to marry him. Now she has two kids, just as she wanted, but she also works all the time to support them and the loser she married. And she spends a lot of her time trying to figure out how to get the heck out of her marriage. Even though you can **"dismount"** that **buck** from your wall (like I did), it takes an awful lot of spackle to cover the wounds. I can't emphasize it enough: don't rush your hunt!

There are, of course, times when you find a good **buck**. When that happens, don't immediately start spending your spare time looking at bridesmaids' dresses. When a lion watches a gazelle through the tall grass, the gazelle's body tenses with fear: it knows something is out there, even if it doesn't know exactly what, or exactly where. It's the same with men. Jumping all over your prey isn't guaranteed to kill him—but it will scare the crap out of him for sure. And that's not what we want to do, especially in public (or private, for that matter). Take it nice and slow and, just like Stella, find your groove.

The Number-One Rule of Hunting

Now, here comes my number-one rule of hunting. NEVER HUNT WITH A **POSSE**! No exceptions. Not, "I had to bring my sister," or, "But I had two tickets." NO, NO, NO. Defying this rule puts you in serious jeopardy. Do I make myself clear?

Let's break it down. If you go hunting with your girlfriends, what will you do? You will buy drinks for one another. You might do a round of shots. You will talk to each other and scan the room together. You might fake-laugh loudly. You will, basically, be trying to draw attention to yourselves *as a group*. In doing so, you turn yourselves into prey. We never want to be prey!

I hear you saying, "But I like going out with my girlfriends. I think I look cooler and less available when I am part of a pack." I get that. But if you want to be hunting, go out alone. If you're part of a **posse**, who do you think you will attract? Not one lone **buck**, but a **herd**. A **herd** that will be attracted to your **posse** as a group—not you as an individual.

Remember, you're hunting for a purpose: to line up a **buck**. When you're out with a **posse** and you've got a **buck** in your sights, guess what can happen? One of your **posse** might have him in her sights, too—or, worse, he's got you *both* in *his* sights. You know why there is such a thing as a *ménage à trois*? Because women hunted with a **posse**. Rather than give up the kill, they shared it so neither one would be left starving in the cold.

If you have a dog at home, try this experiment. First, put one piece of meat on the floor and let the dog go. What happens? He eats the meat. Then, put three pieces of meat on the floor about one inch apart and let the dog go. What happens then? Does the dog choose just one piece of meat? No. He eats all the meat. Get the point?

I know it can be unnerving to go out alone. But it gets easier as you become more and more accustomed to it. Remember—are you out to find a man or to hang out with your friends? If you want to hang out with your friends, fine. But don't hope to kill two birds with one stone. If you try to hunt with a **posse**, both your birds will get devoured.

Practice Makes Perfect

Walking into a place alone on a busy night without feeling awkward is the same as playing a sport well. All it takes is practice and familiarity, both of which you will have gained during the **Off Season**. It's in the **Off Season** that you will visit a variety of sites, find the ones that suit your type of hunting, and cultivate the **kill zone** (see Chapter 2 for more on that). So now, during the **Open Season,** when it counts, you float in gracefully, sit in just the right place and know all the right people. None of the **bucks** need to know that you've been coming there for the past four months. The first time I shot a .22 caliber gun, I was knocked on my ass. After several times, I didn't flinch. I still can't hit the side of a barn, but I look damn calm trying. You see my point? Good training is important.

For the Novice **Hunter**

Going places and doing things alone will be the biggest hurdle for most novice **hunters**. Even experienced **hunters** have moments of overexposure and uncertainty. But if you work on it little by little during the **Off Season**, it really does become easier. Try this: bring a few friends with you somewhere—to a bar, to a party, to a basketball game, to a coffee shop—and while you're all sitting and chitchatting, venture off by yourself for a bit and meet at least one person, male or female. Then rejoin your group. Keep doing this until it feels normal and natural and you wear it like a glove—a hunting glove, to be exact.

Imagine this: you're out and about (without the **posse**), sitting at your favorite restaurant or bar, positioned so you can view the whole scene and chatting with your bartender/

waiter. You see an attractive **buck** and he smiles at you. What do most women do? Either they buy a drink (*blaaaah-hhh!* goes the buzzer! Wrong!) or they look away and giggle (please, ladies, don't giggle). Not only is this the same reaction this buck gets from other **hunters**—and is therefore at best not unique and at worst boring—but giggling sends the message that you aren't in control. Remember, you're the **hunter**. Don't let him think you're the prey.

Don't make it harder than it already is for the poor deer. Think of him standing there in the headlights, scared and intrigued. When he looks at you, *breathe* and then give him a big smile. If you're close enough, just say, "Hello," or, better yet, "Good evening." Maintaining eye contact, offering a nice smile and introducing yourself are the best ice breakers. Think of how you would like to be approached and then reverse it. No one falls for a canned line or a cheesy approach. And there is nothing wrong with your taking the lead. Remember, we are **hunters**, not bait.

After you've made that initial connection, let your personality take over. If you're going to have this **buck** in your life for more than an hour (whether you're hoping to **Bag 'n' Tag** or screw him to your **wall**), you always need to be the true you. If you can't do that, don't even bother setting up a **stand**, because, trust me, you will end up used and tossed aside like **roadkill**. If you are not true to yourself right from the get-go, how can you expect him to be?

But let's not get ahead of ourselves. The first step in successful **hunting** is setting up a good **deer stand**. Turn the page to find out how.

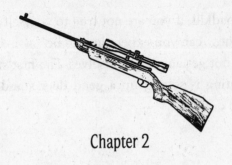

Chapter 2

The Kill Zone and Setting up Your Deer Stand

*L*ocation, location, location . . . well, that sums it up. We **hunt** our prey where the hunting is good. You'd think this is a no-brainer, but this is the first place most **hunters** fail. After getting all fired up about the **Open Season** many girls go running out looking for their **bucks** without any thought about where they're **hunting**. The majority end up stumbling around aimlessly in the urban forest, coming home depressed, tired, hungover and alone. And those who do successfully bring home a kill often wake up the next morning and wish they were alone. So listen up: the most important—but constantly overlooked—factor in successful **hunting** is finding the right spot to lock and load.

In this chapter we will discuss how the type of **buck** you are looking for will determine your **hunting grounds**, which locations are wrong for any planned hunt and how to scout and prepare appropriate **kill zones** during the **Off Season,** so that you hit the ground running when **Open Season** begins April 1. I've also included some helpful examples of **kill zones** for different types of **bucks**, just to start the thought juices flowing.

There's a whole world of bucks out there. Here's a quick guide so you'll know what I'm talking about throughout the book.

- **Velvet Tipped:** This is a young buck who has just sprouted his antlers. Those antlers still have skin lining the hard inner core and the buck, as he matures, has a very strong urge to scrape that skin off on trees or other hard surfaces. Most velvet-tipped bucks are between twenty and twenty-five years of age. You know these bucks: they have an itch that aches to be scratched.

- **4-pointer, 6-pointer and 8-pointer:** Bucks, both my kind and the four-hooved kind, are categorized by age. For our purposes, 4-pointers are men in their 30s; 6-pointers are in their 40s and early 50s; and 8-pointers are in their late 50s and 60s. I have heard about the majestic 10-pointers but don't deal with them directly in my book.

- **The Stag:** Stags can range in age from Velvet-Tipped all the way up to 8-pointer. Stags are strong, secure and attractive. They walk into a room and everyone turns to look at them. The problem with the Stag is that he knows how attractive he is. While he's likely to be graceful and funny, he's also likely to be conceited and selfish. And he's definitely untamable. See chapter 5 for more on The Stag.

Location Rule #1: Men = Shoes

When it comes to hunting, you get what you ask for—or, in our case, look for. This doesn't just apply to finding the right man. Take shoes, for example: if you want quality, comfort, fashion and long-term wearing, you go Neiman Marcus, where you'll pay $400 a pair but get real keepers. If you want hold-me-over-for-the-night trendy heels, you go Payless: $14.99 a pair, and they'll be in the trash or back of your closet before the season changes. There's nothing wrong with either type. What woman doesn't own a pair of cute, cheap shoes she bought because she needed something to match her New Year's dress or a trendy summer sandal? What woman hasn't splurged on Stuart Weitzman or Jimmy Choo because she knew she was getting a classic shoe she could wear for years? You know what I mean. It all depends on what you are looking for. That is why you must choose your **hunting method** before **Open Season** starts, and why you cannot change mid-season. Changing your method will change where you hunt. Try as you may, you will never find a pair of Jimmy Choos at Kmart.

Location is especially critical for **Trophy Hunters**. You don't want to dirty up your **wall** with trash you found at a college "mug and jug" beer joint. You're looking for quality and certain personality traits. Just like deer, each type of man has his preferred regions of roaming. So the first step, one that must be taken during the **Off Season**, is to 1) identify the traits you're looking for, and 2) rank those traits by level of importance. You should check in with your list again and again during the **Open Season** as you continue to **hunt**. You will be surprised at how much your experiences can alter your list, and how much your ideals can change over time.

The List

I know, I know, I can hear you now: "Oh, I have a list already." Really? Do you? Is it an honest, realistic list of "must-haves"? Or is it a man-hating list of past mistakes you have bedded down, a list that has grown over the years to reflect not the man you are looking for but your own past errors in judgment? In management, we reevaluate our goals on a consistent and continual basis. You need to reevaluate the "man of your dreams" list the same way.

I can honestly say that the men I was interested in when I was in college are nothing like those who catch my eye now. First and foremost, when I was twenty, I dated forty-year-olds. Now I live by my mantra, "No scotch passes my lips under twenty-five years old; no man passes my door over twenty-five years old." It's safe to say that if I were still working from the list I had when I was twenty, it would need an overhaul. What about yours? How old is it? You probably need to rethink some of the items.

Sit down and list all the qualities and traits you are looking for in a man. (Don't think this is just for **Trophy Hunters. Bag 'n' Taggers** need a list just as much—if not more. A strong list minimizes the risk of regrettable beer goggle nights.) Now, once you have your list, rank each item by level of importance. You get four points that you cannot live without (be honest and reasonable) and six back-up points that are pretty important but negotiable if your **buck** has everything else going for him.

Piece of advice: don't share the list with others. I know—you want to share it with your girlfriends, and maybe your mom. You want to make sure you're not crazy for saying that "six-figure salary" or "ability to play the guitar" is important to you. But don't do it. This list is for you. Unless you want to date the man your friends want you to date or the one your mom hopes you'll bring home, don't share. Tell your friends and family to shut up and just come to the wedding with a gift if they don't like what or how you're hunting. You're the one who's going to wake up to him every morning, right?

For survival's sake, never, never, never show the list to your captured **buck**. Or any **buck**, even one who is a Bambi to your Thumper. This list is right up there with The Other List. You know what I mean: divulging how many lovers you've had. And haven't you shared that list with a **buck** before? What happened? It came up in fights again and again, right? Same thing here.

Many a **hunter** has thought, "Oh, let me tell him what's on my list. He matches all of it! He will think it's just so great." (Or, "He matches *almost* all of it! He will think it's just so great.") Wrong!!!! I don't have enough fingers on *both* hands to count how many friends have called me up crying after a sharefest with their **bucks**, all saying the same thing: "He said I should be open with him, that not telling him was like lying." You have got to be kidding.

Listen, I made that mistake once. I told a **buck** not only my "must-have" list, but also how many **bucks** I'd captured. Weeelllll, never again. Now I just say, "You're perfect, honey; you blow away any list and I cannot even remember anyone

I was with before you came into my life." (You and I know that is a bit over the top but, hey, it works.)

Once you have your list written down, numbered and circled, what does it tell you? Are you looking for an intellectual? An outdoorsy kind of **buck**, a work–a–holic, a sports buff? Your list will tell you what type of **buck** you're looking for, and therefore where you need to look. Look at an excerpt from my list, for example:

Top Priorities

— physically active/daring

— well traveled and knowledgeable about overseas

— strong hands

Second-tier Priorities

— over 6 feet tall

— very into adventure sports (non-water): horse-manship/skiing/soccer

— busy schedule

— competitive in nature

— good sense of humor

My perfect man basically would be Hugh Jackman in the US Marine Corp. He has all the physical attributes I look for.

Third-tier Priorities

— employed (preferably in a military capacity)

— smart

— self-supporting (but not wealthy—wealthy men need too much attention)

— same political beliefs

— not averse to cigar smoke

— lives alone

— good with animals

— hunts or enjoys eating wild game (this does not
contradict the above trait. You can be good with
animals and still enjoy eating them!)

— speaks another language or with a Southern accent

— is ticklish

. . . And it continues, but that should be enough to make
my point. If you look at my list, it's obvious I am not **Trophy
Hunting.** I'm a **Bag 'n' Tagger.** So I am not going to the latest
scientific expo to find my guy, even though college profes-
sors are kind of cute (and often have strong hands). No, you
will find me hunting in cigar clubs, athletic venues, trails
through the Adirondacks, ski lodges, French restaurants, and
south-of-the-Mason-Dixon-Line military institutions (I'm
not kidding about the accent).

The one item that should be at the top of every **hunter's** list is

— single (not married/engaged/living with someone)

You'd think this would be a no-brainer, but you'd be surprised how many men don't consider not being single a reason to take themselves out of the field. Hunting a **buck** who isn't available is called **poaching**, and I do not recommend it. See Chapter 7 for more.

As a **hunter** you need to decide where your skills and ideals come together. That will point you in the direction of where you will find your best match, regardless of your type of hunting. I am now cultivating my son's military academy for a **kill zone**. Given my interests, I am fortunate that my child wants to be at a military school, so that I can interact with his large, cute and strong teachers, all of whom happen to be retired Army or Marine Corps officers. You may think it sounds manipulative to use your own child in constructing a **kill zone** . . . but as long as he or she is happy, there are no rules against it. As a bonus, every potential **buck** I meet through my son's school already knows about my son—so that's a conversation I don't have to have.

An Elle Real-Life Example:
Elle's **Kill Zones**

To better illustrate this procedure I want you to see how I have recently approached one of my **kill zones**, based on the type of **buck** I am hoping to **Bag 'n' Tag**.

In addition to men in the military, I also happen to enjoy European men. (My reasons for this I am not allowed to fully expand upon due to federal legislation regarding the written word.) Another passion of mine is soccer (European football = European men). I love to watch soccer, and I know a lot about both the U.S. and European leagues. Not only is the game itself exciting, but—icing on the cake— the men are sexy. They have great legs and the endurance for many other stimulating activities.

So, given the above, I targeted my **kill zone** in this way:

1. Buy season tickets for the MLS Red Bulls and go all the time, solo. Not only do I get to ogle the players close up, scream at the referees and drink beer, but I'm also sitting in the stands surrounded by men who have the same passion I do. As happens at all kinds of sporting events, it is easy to start conversations over what flag went down and how American referees wouldn't know offsides if it hit them on the ass.

2. Frequent a typical Irish pub to watch my favorite team (the Gunners) play. Now, I'll be honest with you: it took me a long time to find the right place. But when I did, I made it my business to introduce myself to the bartenders and show them I know and love the sport. That led to making sure they called me when the games were on and staking out "my seat" so that I would have a good vantage point from which to both watch the game and survey the **herd**.

You get my drift. I am building my **deer stand** in that pub, getting acquainted with the people who work there and making myself a regular. Come **Open Season**, all I have to do is perch where I always do and watch as the **bucks** parade on by.

There is only one rule for creating a **kill zone**, and it is very important. Ladies, you must know what you are talking about. Do your homework if you plan to build your **deer stand** in a location that requires knowledge of a certain sport or activity. Use Google; that is what the internet is for. Your success in your **deer stand** will depend on your ability to blend into the surroundings better than the average **hunter**.

This brings me to another point. You are not the only **hunter** out there. In a perfect world you should try to identify locations that are scarce of other **hunters**. Don't be afraid to be creative, to roam outside the box. **Bucks** are creatures of habit but **hunters** cannot afford to be. During the **Off Season** you must prep several different locations. The last thing you want is to find yourself in a rut during **Open Season**. If this happens, immediately find another **kill zone** and jimmy-rig a **deer stand** (it might not be quite as sturdy as it would have been had you built it during the **Off Season**, but it's better than being stuck in a **stand** you don't want to be shooting from).

One more point about being stuck in a rut: if the **herd** sees you constantly (several times a week, or even every day) and you find that you are not excited to be visiting your **stand** or you are using the **kill zone** to blow off steam from work, then you need to take a hiatus from that **stand**. This is especially true for **Bag 'n' Taggers**, for whom dating can move at a quicker pace than it does for **Trophy Hunters**. Deem that **kill zone** a **no-hunt zone** for a period of time. Bringing crankiness or anything less than your A-game to your **stand** defeats the purpose of all the work you did building it, and you will be at risk of becoming a casualty of your own hunt, or, worse, **roadkill**. Cease and desist.

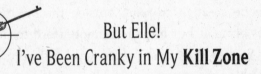

But Elle!
I've Been Cranky in My **Kill Zone**

Should that happen, don't despair. You haven't lost that **kill zone** altogether. When you're ready to approach it in the proper spirit of the hunt, you can go back. And in the meantime, spend some time at one of your other **deer stands**—maybe one in a location you deemed a **no-hunt zone** a few months ago but you now feel ready to investigate again.

Obviously, the sites you choose to build your **deer stands** will be critical to successful **hunting.** And the type of **buck** you are **hunting** should influence where you build your **stands**. Here are some good **kill zones** based on **buck** types:

The Sports Guy

Go to the games! Get season tickets for a sports team or, if you're a single mom, try supporting the local college or high-school team. Volunteer as a coffee mom, supplying coffee to the adults and single dads watching the games. Your son's in the chess club? Your daughter has two left feet? Go to the games together. You won't find a sporty **buck** at the bake-sale committee meeting, that is for sure. If you don't have a child, call the local high school and see if you can do anything to help support the different teams during game days. Maybe you can volunteer coach, if you're sporty yourself.

Another great way to meet a sporty **buck** is to join a sport group. I particularly like road biking. Not only do the guys wear the most incredible tight pants, but also their bodies are incredible. It's okay to let the men in the group help you out with your bike or whatever equipment comes with the sport you opt for. A little bit of neediness here goes a long way, baby! If your **buck** thinks of himself as "the expert," he won't even realize he's in your **kill zone**. One of the biggest pluses for this type of hunt is that you will get in shape and healthy as well.

One note of caution here: make sure you enjoy and understand the sport you're going after. You don't want to sign up for triathlon training if you've never run more than a mile. One of the more klutz-friendly activities I have found that has a great social aspect to it is organized dodge ball. I know there are a number of organized leagues on the East Coast, but if you're in a location where there isn't one, organize it yourself. Organizing an activity is one of the most effective ways to have contact with all those involved—you really get your pick of the **herd** that way.

A few other ideas for the sporty **buck**: triathlons, convention shows (i.e., boat shows, golf shows), charity marathons (you don't have to run these yourself; volunteering is a great way to meet **bucks**). Think outside the box! There are a million different sports out there. Go with what appeals to you.

The Outdoorsy Buck

If you're interested in this type of **buck** you're probably already involved in activities that bring you close to where he roams: hunting clubs, gun shows, boat shows, hiking trails and camping sites. (If you're not already going to these places, take a good look at your list. Outdoorsy **bucks** like having women they can share the outdoors with. If you don't ever want to spend time outdoors, you probably don't want an outdoorsy **buck**.) If you're not finding any **herds** in your day-to-day outdoorsy activities, try joining groups that organize outdoor activities—mountain climbing clubs, orienteering teams, those kinds of things. A quick note of caution: depending on how heavily populated your town is, there can be a lot of "cross-pollination" among different outdoorsy groups. You may have to join a number of different groups so that you aren't always seeing the same people.

Joining a Save the [Some Kind of Animal or Plant Life or The Planet] group is a wonderful way to meet an outdoorsy **buck** *and* do something that is good for the world. If you'd rather eat the animal of the week than save it, try the local shooting club and learn how to hunt for game. Better yet, go to area festivals that highlight wine pairings with wild game. After you enjoy eating the game, you may want to try a co-ed cooking class to learn how to cook it. If you get really good (or already are) you can even host your own cooking class!

The Philanthropist/Business Buck

These **bucks** can be found at charity events, business networking groups, walk-a-thons, clean-up-your-beach weekends, communication workshop retreats or religious retreats, art classes and/or language classes. Join the opera club or get season tickets to your local playhouse. I went so far as to join the UJA so that I could hunt out a nice Jewish banker. (This was before I converted to Judaism, back when I was just an interloping shiksa.) Local protests concerning government issues are also a wonderful way to do self-introductions; just make sure you believe in the cause before you show up and throw your full-fledged support behind it.

A Note on Hunting the Wealthy Buck

I am not an advocate of hunting out the well-off **buck** for the sake of wealth alone. In fact, I am dead set against those types of **hunters**. If you are looking to marry money, go talk to the Millionaire Matchmaker. Hunting with me, you may well hit the "trifecta" (love, looks and money), but I want to remind you that wealth is only one of a number of important criteria. In fact, I always direct **Bag 'n' Taggers** to stay clear of the wealthy **buck**. I have found that when a **buck** has wealth he also has a healthy ego. In my experience, the bigger the assets, the bigger the ego.

Especially beware the wealthy **buck** if you are looking to **Bag 'n' Tag** (see Chapter 4 for more on that). This type of **buck** does not take kindly to being captured and released; in fact, no matter how gently you release him, he often feels unnecessarily rejected. I have seen several, unfortunately, bad reactions to honestly unintended "slights," ranging from the **buck's** unfairly speaking badly about a **hunter** all the way up to the extreme of violence (obviously the violent tendencies were personal-relationship issues, and not connected to this **buck's** wealth). Men who conquer the financial world often have a hard time being conquered themselves. And, to be quite frank, I cannot **Bag 'n' Tag** a guy who spends more time at the manicurist than I do. But to each his own.

The Kill Zone: To Sum Up

The overarching trick to scouting locations for your **kill zone** is twofold. First, identify the type **of buck** you're looking for, and, second, be creative as to where that **buck** might be found. And—and this is very important!—the place/activities should also benefit and complement you. If you are not enjoying what you are doing and where you are doing it, the surrounding **bucks** will not only sense this, but will steer clear. Who wants to be doing something fun with a woman who is miserable and not enjoying herself? Beyond that, hunting is supposed to be fun. Engaging in an activity that isn't fun for the purpose of hunting defeats the purpose.

I've listed below two more of my favorite types of **kill zones.** These are not **buck** specific, so you'll need to pick out the ones you think are most appropriate for your **hunting goals**.

— Volunteering: This is a big one! There are lots of causes and groups out there looking for help: animals and their causes; special-needs adults and children; any political or social problem, either global or local; school events; sporting events (either locally based or local chapters of national groups, like Ride for AIDS); cultural groups—theater, opera, botanical, religious. Volunteering can even be partnered with a vacation ("voluntourism"), which I particularly recommend for **Bag 'n' Taggers.** You go, you help, you bag and then you can leave! It's up to you whether or not you leave behind your correct contact information.

— Nonsport Activities: Cooking classes; any class sponsored by a local university (as long as it's not online); visiting talk shows; becoming a regular at a local restaurant or bar; comedy clubs . . . basically any place where there will be more than two people, provided it is not so girly that **bucks** won't want to be seen there. Read your local paper's neighborhood calendar section for more ideas. If you live in a place that attracts tourists, ask if you can assist in welcoming visitors. I've done that in New York and I have to tell you, it's like giving candy to a five-year-old.

Hunting at Work

Your workplace is never a **kill zone**. There are no exceptions to this rule! **Kill zones** need to be flexible enough that you can stop going to them if you need a break from the atmosphere, or need to avoid a specific **buck** for a little bit. You cannot stop going to work. And having to find a new job because of a hunting mishap is both stressful and unprofessional. Don't hunt at work.

Let's recap. You know what you want to hunt, and you have mapped out the locations in which to do so. Now you have to prep the surroundings. How do you do that? Get yourself known! Visit your **kill zones** often, going to events, restaurants, meetings, etc. Get directly involved with the activities and people that frequent your new **stand**. I like to make the service staff at bars and restaurants my best buddies. I ask them about their lives and really listen to their responses. The more I know about them, and they about me, the more we have to talk to each other about, and the more comfortable I am in their place of business. Also, they'll be my advocates and supporters when I'm hunting—both helping to direct good-looking **bucks** my way, and helping me release a **buck** I'm tired of.

If you remember, I stated in the opening paragraph that "Location, Location, Location" was key to successful hunting. That first "location" was figuring out what type of **buck** you want to be hunting; the second was figuring out where he'll be and which of those spots is a good match for your own skills and interests. The third location is within your chosen **kill zone**, where you choose to build your **deer stand**. You must follow some basic rules:

Vantage point—you need to have an unobstructed view of the field. You should be able to clearly sight all available **bucks**. In the bicycle pack, for example, you want to be in the last tier of riders.

Distance in points—you want to have the greatest opportunity to use your **corn** to attract **bucks** to your **stand**. For example, if you're in an enclosed space, you want to be as far from the restroom as possible. Making your way to and from the ladies' room allows you to survey the room slowly and to entice the **bucks** that have come to graze. Always smile and look left and right as you move to and from your **stand**. You want to look as if you're searching for someone. Never let the **bucks** know they're targets.

No corners—never back yourself against a wall like a caged animal. You want to have open access from all sides—so that the most **bucks** are able to approach you at any given time. Also so that you can escape should a **buck** not understand that you are releasing him.

Chapter 2 is the chapter most heavily invested in the **Off Season**. Even though you can find and set up kill **zones** during **Open Season**, if you need to, this really should be the bulk of your **Off Season** work. I won't lie to you: it's an arduous process. But don't give up. Once you do the Off

Season work, the hard prep work, the rest of the hunt is easy and fruitful.

Online Dating

In the world of **cyber hunting** the rules are not that different, but far more important. When you **cyber hunt**, your goal is not only a successful hunt but also a safe one.

Your first step in **cyber hunting** is exactly the same as in live hunting: make your list of attributes and figure out who you are trying to attract. Once you know that, you need to set up **cyber stands**. Just like potential **kill zones**, not all online dating sites are created equal. You need to figure out which sites are best for your goals. Don't post your profile on every dating site out there just because you can. That's a guaranteed way to waste a lot of time. Whittle your list down to the same number of sites as you would build **deer stands** live. And, just like live hunting, sometimes you'll need to take a break from one particular site. That's okay. If it doesn't feel fresh and new and exciting, give it some space and come back to it when you're ready.

Obviously, you can't look around the room and sight potential **bucks** when you're dating online. Your profile will have to do that work for you, which means that having a well written and clear profile is key. Not only will it dictate the **bucks** you find, but it will also ultimately give you an outline of what to speak about, should you eventually meet in person. Don't put on your profile that you're a soccer fan just because you'd like to meet a European man if you don't know anything about the sport. I guarantee you that if you meet for a drink or dinner, your **buck** will ask you about soccer because that's one of the few things he knows about you. Just like in live hunting: know your territory! And use Google.

One major consideration in **cyber hunting** that doesn't come up as often when you hunt live is false representation. You should never forget that, online, lying is acceptable and most probable. The bullshit detector that we ladies use when hunting in the real world does not work nearly as well online, when we cannot read body language and see the size of a **buck**'s rack ourselves. Do not take anything for face value in the cyber jungle. Skepticism is your safety line.

Okay, enough of the mom speech.

I have had varied success online. I found some real idiots,

one man I almost married, and one who stalked me relent-lessly. It ran the gamut, to say the least. The site I had the most fun with, which I recommend wholeheartedly if you think it's for you, is FarmersOnly.com, which is for rural singles. It reminds me of those movies with mail-order brides being shipped out to the frontier, back when we still had one. These guys are real cowboys: rugged, strong and living in the mountains. My favorite posting was from a guy who wanted a woman who was kind, gentle and a good cook—with strong hands to milk his cows!

To sum up: **cyber hunting** follows most of the same rules as live hunting. Figure out what you're looking for, scout out possible **kill zones**, avoid paying any dues until you know you're looking at the type of **herd** you want to choose from, and then use common sense. And treat everyone like a used-car salesman till you get some references.

Chapter 3

Cultivating the Herd

We came, we saw. Now we conquer. Or, rather, cultivate. Roaming **bucks** are not always easy to come by, whether you're hunting for a date or hunting for real. An inexperienced **hunter** can go days without seeing the firm hide of a **buck** walk by. This chapter delves into how to cultivate and nurture the **herd** for easy pickings.

Making a First Impression

Love at first sight . . . I don't really believe *love* happens that way. However, the idea is not without merit. I do believe that "impression at first sight" is a more accurate take on this old saying. It's sort of like "Don't judge a book by its cover." We all know we're not supposed to, but all of us do. Take this book, for example. The cover was under great debate: What color should it be? What should the central image be? What should the font look like? Who will all those things attract? Are those the people who are going to want to buy it? Will it stand out when it's on a table with fifty other books? Damn, my publisher had a whole team devoted to my book's cover. They're not going to take the chance that people are going to judge it badly based on one quick glance. That's why "impression at first sight" is so important—you don't want to take the chance someone will pass you by because they don't like the look of your cover.

Having said that, if what I wrote in these pages, between the covers, was a bunch of crap, what would it matter how "perfect" the cover was? People would pick it up, flip through it, and then put it back on the table. They're not going to take it home. The next time you're out on the prowl, glance around and watch the actions of other **hunters** in the room. You most likely will see what I have observed: a bunch of women trying to be witty or sarcastically sexy, either laughing too loudly or scowling. Some are even just downright rude and arrogant. Don't kid yourself: **bucks** are just as in tune to the "witchy bitchy" types as everyone else. This type of **hunter** is killing her chances simply by the fact that she is a pain in the neck to be around. She may get attention because of what she looks like, but don't think for a minute that the façade is going to hold up the next morning.

It's not about weight, hair color, natural beauty, height or designer wardrobe. That's all window dressing. What's really important is what's in the window. It's our actions that give real insight to what kinds of people we are. So give up the idea that only the good-looking or overly sexy can attract **bucks**. In fact the most successful hunts I've had have been while I'm still in my equestrian gear or sweat suit, just in from a good workout.

Your parents used to say, "It's what's inside that counts; don't sell yourself short," or something to that effect, and of course you rolled your eyes and said, "Sure, tell that to the football captain." I did, too. But, guess what? They weren't wrong. Sex appeal and likeability do come from within. You cannot buy them, sew them in, tuck them up or plaster them on. How you feel about yourself will shine through any outer trimmings, and there is nothing sexier than an open and confident mind and soul. Attitude, girls, that's what it's all about.

How does this translate into cultivating the **herd**? Simple. If you bounce around your **kill zone** like an arrogant, silly idiot, only the squirrels will come around to see what the ruckus is about. Remember that list you made with all your "must-have" traits? Keep that in mind. Who are you trying to attract? I hope not the good-looking guy in the corner who is also a conceited, shallow idiot. Below you'll find a list of some important techniques to cut the better **bucks** out of the **herd**. These may sound simple, but they are often overlooked and/or ignored.

Smile

You know the Mona Lisa? She isn't exactly a hot chickie, is she? (I think it has something to do with the fact that she doesn't have eyebrows.) But, man, that smile combined with the look in her eyes portrays a very sexy, exciting woman, one who has fascinated men for centuries. Smiling is a way of conveying your own happiness. It signals that you are someone who is fun loving and secure. Do a self-check: how often do you walk around with a look on your face that would scare a small child? If you're not already happy with your life and who you are, and you cannot convey that with a simple thing like a smile, then, hell, who would want to be with you? Men are not women!!!! They don't see a girl with a frown and say, "Ooohhh, she has issues. Let me be with her so I can fix her and make it all better, even to my own detriment!" NO. That's a female M.O. (and one I urge you to get rid of). The **buck** is a free living, upbeat animal who searches out a charismatic, upbeat partner.

Here is a little trick I use all the time. When I am walking around—to work, to meet friends, running errands, going anywhere, really—I sing a song in my mind, usually something upbeat and fun. That keeps a little smile on my face at all times. Even my stress wrinkles fade a bit and my eyes glitter, making me look like I have this great secret inside, just like the Mona Lisa. Those who see me think, "What is she thinking, what does she know?" Being able to convey that without saying a word gives you an edge, big time, over almost anything or anyone else.

Facial Expressions

Being engaged in conversation with someone on one side of the room doesn't mean you're not being peeked at from the other side. Be careful of your facial expressions. If you don't know what I mean, take a look in the mirror and recreate some of the ways you communicate being sad, happy, insulted or angry. You might be surprised at what is looking back at you in the mirror. Sometimes expressions that we think are sexy or funny or attention getting are just scary. And vice versa: sometimes we don't know how good we look when we make a really subtle, simple facial gesture. Practice until you can make your best expressions naturally and easily, without thinking.

Two Elle Real-Life Examples: Making a Good First Impression

Just recently a **buck** sought me out at my cigar club (my best and favorite **kill zone**). This **buck** is a fine catch: wealthy, handsome and honorable! He told me that he remembered me from more than two years ago, from an event at the cigar club, at which I was running around playing hostess extraordinaire. I had only a vague recollection of him and maybe said three words to him at the time. But he'd been watching me and had liked what he'd seen. So always make sure you're presenting yourself well. You can reap those benefits for literally years to come.

This advice holds very true in the case of bad situations as well. I'm a pretty easygoing lady; it takes a lot to insult me. But once, again at my club, a total ass of a man pulled me aside and asked what it would take to have me "do a three-way" with him and a friend. Now, mind you, I was wearing a business suit and looked totally respectable. I have no idea what gave him the idea I'd be into "doing a three-way" with him and his buddy. But even though I was very offended, I was also conscious that we were in my **kill zone** and there were other **bucks** grazing nearby. So I simply removed his hand from my arm and said very sweetly and with a smile, "The first thing would be your wife's permission. Maybe you should put your wedding band back on the finger where your tan mark is and give her a call." Then I wished him a good evening and walked away.

I could easily have yelled at that man or caused a scene. But that would have brought me unwanted negative attention. As it turned out, a gentleman sitting within hearing distance was so impressed by my conduct that he approached me several days later and asked me to dinner. We are just friends now, but we had a lovely meal, and it's always nice to see this **buck** at the club. Remember: it's not always who you're talking to at the moment, it's also who's watching you do it.

One other point from that story: after I walked away from

the insulting **buck**, I informed club management what had occurred. That man was never again seen in the club. That's
why it's important to spend the **Off Season** prepping your
kill zone (see Chapter 2). If you run into a sticky situation,
you're in a good position to put up fences around the offend-
ing **buck**; you don't have to go to the trouble of finding a new
kill zone or building a new **deer stand**.

Small Talk and Introductions

The typical **buck** is usually a little bit reserved. Remember:
you are hunting him, not the other way around. After you've
smiled and made eye contact, maybe had a very casual
encounter at the bar, the next step—and I think the most
powerful—is a self-introduction. The self-introduction is
"first impression and between the book covers" rolled into
one opportunity—you're still unknown enough to the **buck**
that he's reacting to you instinctually and paying a lot of
attention to your outer package, but you're going to give

him a quick taste of your inner personality. Don't waste this important moment with a lame intro.

Have you ever been to the circus? Before anything else happens—before the clowns come out juggling and the trapeze artists start swinging and the tiger-wranglers start cracking their whips—the ringleader comes out and says, in a booming voice, "Here comes the great, the wonderful, the magnificent **hunter** . . . Ellllllllllllle!" He doesn't come out and say, "Uh, yeah, here's Elle, thanks." Can you imagine the big difference in applause if he did? Make sure you are your own ringleader. Make it a point to be the first to introduce yourself. If you wait to be introduced by someone else, or wait for the **buck** to speak up first, you run the risk of an unenthusiastic opening.

Handshake

Hunters like the upper hand. You want to be in control; you are the **hunter**, not the prey. A firm handshake is always a good sign of character, so make sure you have your hand out and ready, and make note of the shake you get back. If it's flimsy, that's a clue to the type of **buck** you're shaking. The reverse holds true, too: beware the painfully hard grip. I am also a big fan of the two-handed shake, gently grasping the back of the **buck's** hand. It's different from what most women do, plus it's a sign of intimacy. Smile and say your name in a strong and clear voice as you shake firmly. And that brings us to the most important piece of this introductory exchange. . . .

Eye Contact

Now, some people believe you can bewitch or hypnotize a **buck** by keeping him in your gaze. Like all the sayings I have mentioned in this chapter, this idea has some truth to it. Maintaining a natural eye contact with your prey is key. But please note: the eye contact *must* be natural. Psychotically staring at your **buck** will frighten him away. Have you ever been stared at? I have and, wow, it gave me the heebie jeebies. Nothing screams, "Hey, I am a stalker!" like staring. It's the perfect way to ward someone off.

So, eye contact. *Gaze*, don't stare. Your expression should be natural and soft. Keeping natural eye contact with your prey also allows you to look into his eyes. If he cannot match your gaze, beware! That is often a sign that your **buck** is hiding something, like a wife or improper intentions. Or it could mean he is shy and insecure. Either way, not making eye contact is a telltale sign that your **buck** has some issues you'll have to address later on. Time to ask yourself . . . do you want to? (I know what you're thinking: shyness is a much less serious issue than a secret wife. But think about it a little more: even if you coax a timid **buck** to open up around you, you'll have to deal with his lack of social confidence in every other situation. Is that something you want to deal with?)

The other important part of making eye contact is that it separates you from other **hunters**. Most women are insecure and have a hard time matching a gaze, so when you do, you become more alluring, confident and engaging. And the **buck** can see your beautiful eyes. Every woman has beautiful eyes. Think about it. There are unfortunate noses, thin hair, too-strong jawlines—but have you ever seen anyone and thought, "Wow, she has ugly eyes?" No. So let your **buck** see yours.

One parting note about this technique: just as you practice making attractive faces in the mirror, practice making eye contact while lying. Until you are an accomplished liar, your eyes will always give you away. My mother will tell you how good a liar I am, but that has come with years of practice.

Lying

I do not encourage **hunters** to lie as a matter of course. Being truthful is essential to being secure and honest with yourself, and ultimately an essential part of a secure and honest relationship. However, in these early stages of the hunt, I do recommend a slight fib about certain personal details. These include:

— number of sexual partners

— finances

— family details and relationships

— personal contact information

— names of ex-lovers/husbands

— weight or the fact that you recently dropped 20 lbs.

— real hair color

— what you look like in the morning

If your **buck** is a keeper, he will find out all this information in due course (except maybe real hair color and number of sexual partners. A little mystery goes a long way, even in marriage.). But you don't want to give a full account of your meddling family's nagging ways or the miracles Weight Watchers can work too soon.

Body Language

CIA and FBI profilers will tell you they can tell almost everything about a person by his or her body language. I completely agree. Your posture, hand gestures, head tilting, etc., are all very indicative of who and what you are. Sit up straight. Not straight-on-the-edge-of-your-seat-like-you're-waiting-for-a-bomb-to-go-off, but straight relaxed. Drop your shoulders down your back and engage your abs. Imagine a cord pulling you up from the very top of your head. (Yes, that is yoga advice I'm giving you.) Good posture is not only crucial to how **bucks** will view you now but will also deter uncorrectable bad posture later on in life. No one wants a hump when she is sixty.

How are your legs positioned? Are you sitting like a jock with an itch, or a lady? Are you a dangler or a foot swinger? You want to look comfortable and relaxed, but remember that your goal is to put your femininity on display. You are not at a hippie sit-in. Be conscious of your positioning.

And, speaking about positioning, I do not care how "cool

and sexy" the open-legged, panty-free sitting position of the lovely Ms. Sharon Stone in *Basic Instinct* was. You are not Sharon Stone, nor are you in a movie. If you attempt her trick, it will come off more like the Britney Spears version: the eewww-look-at-that-nasty-Brazilian-shave shot captured by the paparazzi. So keep your legs closed until you are in a position to open them for a useful purpose.

Herd Cultivation

The techniques above are critical for your **herd cultivation**. Practice them at home until confident, smooth motions come naturally and easily. When you are at your **kill zones**, you will use these motions as **corn** to attract **bucks**. And make no mistake: you want to throw out the **corn** all around you, not only to those **bucks** you feel interested in. Because—and this is important—you aren't cultivating individual **bucks** but rather the **herd** in its entirety. The more **bucks** notice you, the more highly you will be thought of. Every **buck** is interested in a **field of corn** he knows his fellow **bucks** are interested in, too.

Prepping your **kill zone** and **cultivating your herd** go hand in hand. As you do one, the other should follow. You should think of yourself as acting as the hostess with the mostess in the place(s) you have chosen. You are not scoping! Not only is that obvious, but it is also tacky. And everyone does it. You want to be perceived as different. That way, **bucks** who are used to being scoped—and are often arrogant about and immune to it—will be intrigued.

I believe there is some literature out there regarding "old cow/new cow" syndrome. Well, **cultivating your herd** is how you set yourself up as "new cow." But you are not a hunted new cow, sitting in a field waiting to become hamburger! You are using your **corn,** and your prey's curiosity and interest, to lead him right up to your **deer stand**. If you do this right, the **buck** thinks he's in control. That's where you want him. Now he is yours for the taking.

This part of hunting—**herd cultivation**—is really fun. Be careful. You can get carried away with it. I have girlfriends who, once they have mastered **herd cultivation**, abandoned their **Trophy Hunting** goals to do some **Bag 'n' Tagging**. Beware! When you see how easy properly prepared hunting can be, sometimes greed sets in. Even Mother Theresa could have been swayed by all the attention a powerful, confident, aloof **hunter** can garner if she understands and executes **herd cultivation** correctly. If you're **Trophy Hunting,** enjoy that attention for a while but remember your intentions. You should not switch methods during the **Open Season**!

If you're **Bag 'n' Tagging** this season, go for it! But you **Bag 'n' Taggers** need to look out for a few things as well. You are at risk of excessive cockiness and arrogance. Remember, the best **hunters** are humble about their success. Also, somewhere down the line you may find yourself so inundated with **Bag 'n' Tag** opportunities that you start to feel overwhelmed. Don't worry. Every so often even a skilled **hunter** needs to put down her gun and remind herself of who and what she is, and what she is looking for. (This is one of the main reasons why we follow a season; it helps us avoid gluttony and take some time for ourselves.) If you ever start to feel like you're taking your success for granted during **Open Season**, it's fine to take a week or two off before picking up the hunt again.

In Closing—Two Final Points

Two more items need mentioning. The first is manners. Proper behavior and politeness are two of my pet peeves, and I will come back to them again and again throughout this book. The rudeness I have witnessed and experienced out there in our "civilized" society is downright appalling. If you notice a man is not holding doors, offering seats, or doing whatever else your grandmother would have considered no-brainer gentlemanly behavior, why would you think he'd be different to you, in or out of bed?

The same goes for us. If a man sees a woman constantly accepting pleasantries and never saying thank you or you're welcome, why should he feel compelled to act appropriately? As a mom I have to ask the generation before me, "What did you all do, raising your sons not to respect women?" And it's not just men who are the problem. Dads giving everything to their little girls created a bunch of "gimme gimme bitches" who are just as distasteful. Always have a "kindness on your lips," in all ways.

One of my favorite tricks to use when I am out—and it

works like a charm—is the Southern thing. I've spent a lot of time with my Southern friends while visiting South Carolina during hunting seasons, and I've picked up the Southern accent and charm like a native. After one single malt, you can't even tell I'm a Yankee. And let me tell you, "Thank you, sir," and "Thank you, darlin'," have gotten me very far in **cultivating** many a **herd** and tagging many a **buck**. I suggest you spend some time finding and practicing your own special way of showing "kindness and gentility."

The second point I want to mention here is hunting attire. This topic is covered in much more detail in Chapter 8, but here's the quick CliffsNotes version: be comfortable and never forget that the clothes make the woman. If you dress like a hooker, expect to be paid. If you dress only designer, head to toe, expect to be labeled "high maintenance." Proper **gear** and appropriate attire are critical to the hunting process. Before going out there, take the time to read Chapter 8: Hunting Gear.

I cannot think of anything that isn't **cultivated**. The economy (though not always with success), the land, relations (whether they are political or social), business contacts, even world peace. As parents we cultivate relationships with our children; as employees we do the same with our colleagues and employers. So, considering how much effort we put into cultivating every other aspect of our lives, isn't it shocking that so few people think about **cultivating** prospective lovers? To quote a farmer, proper cultivation results in a higher yield of better quality. **Hunters** of the world, your **cultivation** work is never done. Do the bulk of it in the **Off Season**, refine your methods and strategies during the **Open Season**, and you will soon find that it comes so easily and naturally that your efforts will spill over into every other aspect of your life. Who knows? You might even be able to achieve world peace.

Chapter 4

Trophy Hunting:
The Art of Mounting

Most little girls grow up thinking they will meet Prince Charming and live happily ever after. In reality, they usually end up with one of the Three Little Pigs or, worse, the Big Bad Wolf. That's why we can't rely on fantasy to determine our destiny. A woman must be able to **bag** the big one and **mount** him on her **wall** herself.

Over the years, women have put off marriage and child-bearing for their careers. They have used their intellectual power to rise to CEO status, even venturing into the presidential realm. And yet these are the same women who complain over drinks with their **posse** that there isn't a straight guy to be found or that they're all "married jerks." If I had a dollar for every time I heard that, I wouldn't have had to write this book. Think about it, girls. If you are passed over for a promotion at work, what do you do? You probably call your boss a jerk, but then you either work harder to make sure the promotion is yours the next time, or you start sending out your résumé, looking for a company that will promote you right now. But do you just take it and whine? I don't think so! So why would you do that over a man?

The goal of **Trophy Hunting** is to find a **buck** that you can **mount** on your **wall**. In other words, you're looking for a **buck** who wants to be married or in a committed relationship. This **mounting** should be based on trust, love and respect. With that understood, some of your tactics will be very different from the tactics you would use to **Bag 'n' Tag**.

One of the major mistakes I see women make all the time while searching for a **Trophy** is that they waste their time. Ask yourself: when you interview for that perfect job to further your career, do you schedule multiple interviews or do you wait for one to take its course until you schedule another? Of course you interview for several jobs simultaneously. Well, so should it be with dating. Date, date, date until you find a **buck** that's worth the second, third and fourth date. And even then, keep dating. Don't sit around waiting for the phone to ring or, worse, for a proposal. It is extremely common for women to spend two, three or ten years dating the same **buck,** and in the end, they end up with empty **wall** space.

Precapture

Precapture is the moment at which you have a **buck** in your sights and the two of you have begun dating. You did everything you were supposed to during **Open Season** and now you've got a good one taking **corn** from your hand. During this time, you need to realize one important thing and never forget it. The **buck** is looking at you as two distinctly different women. First, he sees the exciting sexy you to whom he is attracted. Make no mistake, he wants to get into that woman's pants (side note—it is your job to make sure that his wanting continues for a while yet). But the **buck** is also starting to see you as a person who might share his life, take care of him and give him children (or take care of the ones he's got). Keeping that in mind, it's important to say please and thank you, stay sober while out with his friends and always refrain from using foul language. All of this translates into WIFE, MOTHER. The same goes for your attire. Keep it tailored and classy.

During **precapture**, you really should not be dating only one **buck**. Keeping it to one **buck** at a time in the very beginning puts added pressure on you to make that capture work, and you lose the carefree, fun feeling that **hunting** should bring you. But, to be very clear, dating multiple **bucks** means just that: dating, as in dinner outings. It pains me, the modern **hunter**, to admit this hard and sad truth, but true it is: sleeping with your **buck** too soon is crossing a very fine, dangerous line that has dashed the hopes and dreams of many a **hunter**.

During **precapture,** your **buck** is a lusty animal who has **rutting** at the front and center of his mind. You need to caress and guide that lust into an emotional need for you. You can't accomplish this by manipulation or playing games, as many a "dating expert" has suggested. You just need to keep your legs together long enough for your **buck** to tell you how he feels about you. I tell women all the time: if you want him as a **Trophy**, don't bed the **buck** down until a minimum of two months into the **precapture**. By the way, this includes all oral sex, anal sex and anything that resembles genital rubbing. I am a Republican. I do not play fast and loose with the definition of sex. You are looking for a **Trophy**, not trouble.

Speaking of trouble, during this **precapture** time you need to be wary of getting caught "double-dipping." When you date multiple **bucks**, please, please, *please* keep the geography separate. I always keep outings with different **bucks** far apart for safety's sake. As you continue to spend time with your multiple **bucks**, you should be able to find out where each of them likes to roam. Steer clear from those known areas when you are entertaining a different **buck**. Accidentally getting caught will not spur a **buck** to get more interested (the exception is the **stag**, and if you are **Trophy Hunting** you should not be hunting **stags,** anyway; see Chapter 5 for more on that). Getting caught with another **buck** only results in enormous tension and arguments. Avoid the drama at all costs.

Getting Caught
with a Different **Buck**

If you do happen to get caught by a **buck** with one of his competitors, do not address it at the time. You've seen this happen in countless chick flicks. The scenes are always awkward and uncomfortable, right? (Sometimes they're supposed to be "funny," but only for the viewer. The humor comes at the expense of the **hunter**.) Quickly and graciously get out of the situation—do not feel that you need to explain yourself! If the **buck** who caught you demands an explanation the next time you see him, simply tell him that you did not realize you were seeing him exclusively, and that if that is something he would like to do, you are open to discussing it. (Try to hold this conversation off until **Open Season** ends, if you can—it's much more natural and healthy to begin exclusive dating during the **Off Season**.)

So, you're in **precapture** with a **buck**. After a date, the longest you should ever wait for a call is one week. Obviously, don't sit at home waiting for a call—or make plans only with your **posse** and keep your phone on the table so you can answer it the minute your **buck** calls. Keep hunting. If he doesn't call after a week, mentally release him and turn your attention toward one of your other targets.

Now, let's say you really like this **buck**. He's far and away more impressive than any of the other members of the **herd** you've been **cultivating**. And he calls on day eight. You think, "He's only one day late! He's probably been busy at work, or had friends in town." I will let you use your judgment here, but short of death of a family member or his ending up in the hospital, I would not return a phone call made more than seven days after I'd gone out with a **buck**. **Precapture** is similar to disciplining a child or training a dog. If you let **bucks** take advantage of your **corn** once, they will do it again and again, each time taking a little bit more. Until you are in a committed relationship, you have no reason to compromise or adjust your values, and the **buck** should know that.

But if you feel this **buck** is really special, I do think it's okay for a **hunter** to reach out with a **corn** offering. Pick up the phone and call him. Yes, you heard me. It's fine for a woman to call a man. It's how you call and when that is more the issue. Just call once, usually seven to ten days after you've seen the **buck**, leave a casual message, and leave it at that. If you don't get a response in two days, retract the **corn** and move on.

Releasing Other **Bucks**

About moving on: when you start having a preference for one of your **bucks** over the others, be gentle when you release your other **bucks** back into the wild. The last thing you want is negative talk about you spreading through the urban forest. And make no mistake: the **bucks** do talk to one another. (You thought it was just **hunters** who talked? You're wrong.) You do not want bad publicity getting around your **kill zones**—even if the rumors are untrue, they create bad karma you want to avoid.

When I release a **buck,** I keep it very simple and to the point. I avoid clichés like, "It's not you, it's me," or being so straightforward that I tell the released **buck** that I have found someone better (even if you don't actually say "better," they can read between the lines). Avoid burning your **buck**. I like to say that my life is going in another direction that I feel I need to explore, and that to remain true to myself I have to walk that path alone. I find that giving a reason that sounds deep and philosophical tends to limit protests. It's difficult to argue against something that doesn't have concrete points to rebut.

One final point about releasing a **buck**: once you have freed him back into the urban woods, he's gone. You cannot string him along "just in case" things don't work out with the **buck** you're committing to, or for those times you need a little ego boost. And you certainly can't pull a jealous move on him should you discover some other **hunter** has snatched him up. All three of those things will not only wear you out emotionally, but they have the potential to destroy your good image in the urban forest—an image you need to maintain in order to find the true **buck** of your hunting dreams.

So, back to the **buck** you've decided to commit to. Eventually, it will be the right time for the horizontal mambo (or vertical, depending on your preference). I cannot tell you exactly when that time will be. Each **hunter**—and each relationship—has its own time frame, and the right time evolves naturally depending on the feel of each specific relationship. However, you should feel that there is a sense of intimacy and seriousness in the relationship before sex comes into play. If you find yourself second-guessing whether it's the right time, then I guarantee you it is too soon. Listen to your good sense.

My father always said, "a lady in the kitchen, a whore in the bedroom." In my dad's time, apparently no one was screwing up against the kitchen sink (side note: what a great way for your **buck** to see you as he walks in the door—you standing there in his work shirt and heels (forego the underwear; it just makes it complicated), with the aroma of a delicious meal wafting in the air). While it's okay to be the prude in the bar when he is hanging out with the boys, don't let that prude follow him into the bedroom. Sex should be sexy, steamy, fun and adventurous. This is the most intimate time you will spend with your **buck**—open up and explore each other! Don't be scared. If you are unsure of yourself, simply ask for directions. We are women, remember—we don't have a problem with that. No man can resist a woman who looks up at him and asks him how he enjoys oral sex. And every man likes this done in a different way; I have yet to use the same technique twice. Even if you think you're an expert, try asking for a little direction. You'll make him feel special and get a few new tricks for your bag.

I'm not suggesting you do anything that makes you uncomfortable. That would undermine the security you feel with this **buck**. If he persists in asking for something that makes you uneasy while you are being intimate, simply say no. Later, when you are both clothed, revisit his request. You need to be able to discuss intimacy with your **buck** and be honest about what you are comfortable with. If your **buck** continues to ask for something you have told him makes you uncomfortable, that may be a deal breaker. Deal breakers are always a bummer, especially if you really like everything else about your **buck**, but the sooner you find out about any particular oddball sexual requests, the better. You want to be able to get out of the relationship before you get any more deeply entrenched. (And, more important, deal breaking in the bedroom may also be an indication of other non-negotiables to come.)

Elle's Secret Sex Tip

So, you've gotten to bed, you've pleased your **buck** (and he's pleased you right back, I hope), and now you're lying together in a state of bliss (again, I hope!). Believe it or not, **bucks** are very vulnerable after sex. Not in the same way that we are, exactly, but they are in a weakened state. Here's my post-sex secret weapon. If it's done with an honest intention, it never fails to show your **buck** that you care for him, and that you're happy to have done what you've just done.

Rather than going in for the cuddle (which really just screams, "I am vulnerable!"), try this. Get up, naked. Don't cover up. He's been waiting a long time to see you like this. Let him get a good, long look. Move naturally to the bathroom and get a nice, fluffy white face towel (see Chapter 8: part of your **Off Season** gear preparation is to buy half a dozen soft white washcloths to keep in the bathroom). Soak it in hot water. Wring it out and bring it back to the bedroom (or whichever room you've ended up in). Very casually, say something sweet to him in a soft voice and while you are speaking use the face cloth to clean his genitals, all around. Use both hands. This achieves two objectives. First, it makes your **buck** feel taken care of. Second, it protects your 300-count Egyptian cotton sheets.

But Elle! I Slept with Him, and He Hasn't Called!

If, after you've slept together, your **buck** doesn't call, or just disappears, three things could have happened. You might have miscalculated and slept with him too soon. You might have misjudged him as a **Trophy Buck** when in actuality he was a **stag**. **Stags** sometimes pretend to be **Trophy Bucks** in order to pick up the **Trophy Hunters**. They have a particularly vicious type of M.O.: coming in strong and running just as quickly, leaving the hunter vulnerable and broken **roadkill**. (See Chapter 5 for more on the **stag**.)

The third thing that might have happened—and this may be hard to face—is that your **buck** might have found someone else. Whichever is the reason (and you may not know—you may not ever find out), don't chase him or wait by the phone for him to call you. Once you've slept with him, give him two days to call, maximum. If you don't hear from him, give your gun a polish, head back to **your deer** stand, and don't look back—ever.

Let's assume your **buck** calls within the appropriate time frame. So, you're having sex (side note: refrain from using the term "making love" with your **buck** right away; it contributes to the "**deer in the headlights**" syndrome) and dating regularly, and the **Open Season** is closing. Continue dating your **buck** through the **Off Season** and see how things go as you make your way through the **Tension Days**. All the while, keep asking yourself if this is what you want. Do not ask him how many children he wants or where he would like to live. These are discussions for after the commitment, not during **precapture**. During **precapture**, you should be relaxed, enjoying the fun and excitement, and thinking about whether you think your **buck** is a keeper. Don't worry about whether he likes you. Do you like how he acts? Is he respectful, even when angry? Zero in on his flaws and see if you can get comfortable with them. I keep a list of pros and cons on the refrigerator. After each date, I write down two pros and two cons. I don't think about the list at work or as I'm falling asleep or while I'm out with my **buck**; I just keep it going as we continue dating. Then I evaluate after each **Tension Day** to see where I stand. If it's a good catch, it will bloom all by itself into a perfect **mount**.

An Elle Real-Life Example: Wasting Valuable Open Season Time

Don't waste the opportunity of a new **Open Season** on unsubstantiated hope. Let me explain by example. I once dated a guy who was younger than I was. We became very close and entered into a committed relationship. By our second year together it became apparent, to me, at least, that we were heading for marriage. Surprisingly, I was actually okay with that (it's only happened twice in my life). Though this **buck** had met my whole family, including my son, he somehow just couldn't figure out how to introduce me to his family. There was always an excuse. Either they were not around (they lived in Florida half the year) or someone was dying (really!) or he didn't want to hear negatives from them that could taint our wonderful relationship. I convinced myself that he must have issues with them. After all, why else wouldn't he have introduced me? HA! What a bunch of crap. I finally found out the truth: I was a recent convert to my new religion, and the family did not feel that I was "Jewish" enough for them. I also discovered that this idiot **buck** was only "practicing" on me, as I was not Jewish enough for his future children, either. I wasted two years of my mid–30s because the only issue he had was about marrying me. I dumped him the day before I Mikva'd (took the ritual bath to complete my conversion) and never looked back.

Now, just a side note: the nut stalked me. He would call me before each religious holiday, he would call my friends to see how and what I was doing, and he even demanded, via an email, visitation rights with my son (who was not his son— my son's father already had visitation rights!). This **buck** went to all my **kill zones** and made them his. I had to change every-where and everything I did. It was awful. He even called me while he was on his honeymoon, which occurred exactly one year after we broke up. I finally had his rabbi ask both him and his new wife to leave me alone. One week later I received another call—from a woman who asked my name, then immediately hung up. I never heard from him again.

Obviously, that time a higher power was protecting me from a second **failed mounting.** But even though I was ultimately glad not to have to pry that **buck** from my **wall**, I felt the sting. No one likes wasting time.

When You're Ready for the Next Step . . . but He Might Not Be

If, once you are in a committed relationship, you have doubts or just get that feeling that your **buck** is giving you too many excuses, don't give him an ultimatum. Rather, speak to him as a mature adult about your feelings. Tell him you think you and he make a great couple and you would like to have a further commitment from him. See how he reacts. Ask him for a time frame, for the amount of time he needs to think about it. If what he asks for sounds reasonable, agree. If it doesn't, negotiate down. And then give your **buck** that time to adjust his behavior.

Whatever you do, once you've said your piece, don't— don't!—hold on forever with crossed fingers. That will just lead to anger and resentment, which will seep into the relationship, causing friction that will overshadow any progress toward getting a proposal or commitment. Be patient and act as you normally would. Don't be passive-aggressive or make hints about rings or cohabitation or friends you have whose boyfriends have just asked them to take the "next step." Be a good girlfriend. And then, when time is up, it's up. If he hasn't agreed to the commitment you asked for, you need to let him go. Either he will go his way (in which case, good riddance—he didn't love you the way you deserve to be loved) or he will become overwhelmed with a feeling of loss and track you down, begging to marry you (in which case, hesitate momentarily for effect, then make sure he has a ring with him). It's not easy, I know, but it makes your life manageable so that you don't waste your time.

Just for reference, I would never give a **buck** more than six months to make the commitment after you have had a conversation about marriage. This is ample time for a relationship to build a foundation. To be more specific I would base the proposal timeline on an age scale:

20–27 years old	Six months from the commitment conversation
28–33 years old	Five months from the commitment conversation
34–38 years old	Three months from the commitment conversation
38 and older	Honey, if there is no movement two months after the commitment conversation, ship him out

Never go longer than a full year—one **Open Season** and **Off Season** cycle—from the time of the commitment conversation to see that commitment materialize.

Should you release your **buck** back to the wild, don't be depressed. There's another **Open Season** right around the corner. Get right back out there. But make sure you wait for the **Open Season**. If you release during the **Off Season**, take the time until **Open Season** to recalibrate your hunting grounds. Get your **hunting gear** in order. **Cultivate your herd**. Haven't you heard? Some states are overpopulated with deer. Rest assured, a better **buck** will come into your sights. Just stick to the plan.

The best thing about the **Off Season** is that it keeps you out of your own way. There's a saying that "you have the relationship you want; otherwise you wouldn't have it at all." Well, that's true. If you keep holding on to your most recent **buck** *or* your old feelings for him, you won't see the man of your dreams if he comes up and taps you with his antlers. Use the **Off Season** to deal with that baggage, so that you can enter the **Open Season** with it behind you.

Getting rid of baggage isn't always easy. It may require therapy, exercise or a new sport or hobby. Or it may just be that you need to admit to yourself that you were duped. That's okay. We're all human and sometimes we don't see the forest for the handsome tree. Don't waste your time on anger or self-pity. Learn from the lesson and go forward. Reread Chapter 3, remind yourself how to build a sturdy **deer stand** and **cultivate a herd** and, when **Open Season** rolls back around, get back out into the woods!

Chapter 5

Bag 'n' Tag: The Art of Catch and Release— Plus a Word about the Stag

Bag 'n' Tag is my game. It's an animalistic, carefree way of looking at relationships. Take note: I say *relationships* on purpose. **Bag 'n' Tag** is not, and never should be confused with, the damning one-night stand. A one-night stand is **Bag 'n' Tag** gone very, very wrong (see sidebar, later in this chapter).

Bag 'n' Tag is very simple in concept. It's a mutual agreement between **hunter** and prey to enjoy the hunt, with the understanding that: a) the **hunter** will release the prey back into the urban forest and b) the **buck** will be available for capture again in the future. If done correctly it's a win-win.

Think "green" regarding **Bag 'n' Tagging**. You came, you enjoyed and then you didn't leave any garbage behind. Like not littering when you go camping, get it?

Bag 'n' Tagging is an art form and not for all **hunters**. **Hunters** who have recently been through a bad breakup or are in that "I hate men" state of mind (you know what I'm talking about—we all go through it from time to time) shouldn't attempt this method of hunting. **Bucks** are not like alcohol; you cannot cure an overindulgence with a little "hair of the dog." If you have recently been dumped, the only cure is some time out of the forest, cleaning your wounds and not your gun. To go **Bag 'n' Tagging** while you still feel like **roadkill** will only end one way: with a total destruction of the **hunter** and her future skills. Trust me on this.

Because **Bag 'n' Tag** does not result in a serious commitment or life partner, some women think of it as an escape from "real life." But that's not what it is at all. **Bag 'n' Tag** is a way of life that offers fun and sex without emotional or family baggage. I will warn you: it's not for the faint of heart or a jealous type of **hunter**. You can't embrace this type of hunting if you are looking to fall in love. When the emotionally weak or unskilled **hunter** attempts this method she usually ends up on the pointy part of the **buck's** horns. You cannot mistake the carefree fun **Bag 'n' Tagging** affords for "attachment." If you let your guard down as you let your skirt up, you'll become **Bag 'n' Tag roadkill,** and I promise you, there is no more devastating kind.

But Elle! I've Just Been Through a Breakup, I Can't Sit Home and Cry Anymore.

When I was a young **hunter** I went through a mutual breakup with a fine-looking **velvet-tipped buck**. This **buck** was sexy and sleek, and he knew just how to make me sigh. It was as though he had the "Elle manual." After we went our separate ways, I was smart enough to nurse my wounds before going back on the hunt. Now that didn't mean I wanted to be alone and without good-looking men, so I did what many **hunters** do when laid up with injuries: I hung out with my gay friends. That gave me the time away from anything tempting while still keeping me out, about and in the company of some of the hottest men I have ever laid my eyes on. (Of course, my eyes were the only thing that got laid with that crowd. But that was the point.) After a few months I was ready to hit my **deer stands** again, gun in hand.

In case you didn't get my point above, let me spell it out: **Bag 'n' Tagging** is not "rebound hunting." There is no such thing as "rebound hunting." If you are brokenhearted, no type of hunting can cure you. You will need to work through things on your own. Each of us has her own way of healing. My method might not work for you. As a hunter you will need to create a healing process that you respond to. And then use it!

If you have "jealousy issues," you should not **Bag 'n' Tag**. This method of hunting is all about non-ownership of the **buck**. He ain't yours, so you cannot lay claim to him when other **hunters** sniff around. **Bag 'n' Tagging** is the equivalent of sexual time sharing, without the Marriott logo. It really is an art form. Feelings of jealousy and ownership are natural, and part of our human makeup (plus they're an ego thing). It can take years of practice to recondition a **hunter** to eliminate those feelings. But, trust me, they have no place in the world of **Bag 'n' Tagging**. Going out and hunting down a buck for a **Bag 'n' Tag**, stating all the while, "Hey, I am not into commitment, let's just enjoy each other now and again," and then going all psycho on him when he doesn't ask you to meet his mother—that's animal cruelty, plain and simple.

Self-knowledge and honesty are really important here. If you even suspect you want to **Trophy Hunt**, spend a long time thinking before you decide to spend a season **Bag 'n' Tagging**. The worst **roadkill** I see is **Trophy Hunters** who pretend they're **Bag 'n' Taggers**. You'll lose your dignity quicker than an accidental shotgun blast.

Okay, so are you still with me? I've given all my warnings. I am no longer responsible for any heartbreak that occurs during **Bag 'n' Tagging**. Disclaimer over.

Reasons to Bag 'n' Tag

Welcome to my world of **velvet-tipped bucks, four pointers** and the elusive **stag**. I invented this method of hunting simply because I love men, and there are so many different types to love. It's like shoes. You need more than one pair: shoes for working out aren't the same as the shoes you wear to work or the shoes you wear on summer weekends.

I know what you're saying: "But, Elle, you told me to make a list of all the criteria I'm looking for while hunting.

My list won't get me sneakers and stilettos!" That may be true, but let me ask you this: how many pairs of black high heels do you own? More than one, right? And each one has a different feel and look. How much more boring would your wardrobe be if you were only allowed to have one pair of black heels?

Just as different outfits dictate different-looking shoes, so my life and moods dictate different **bucks**. I share each separate area of my life with a different **buck**—or go it alone, if I so choose. The key is maintaining a relationship with many **bucks** simultaneously.

When I first started this type of hunting, I was subjected to much criticism. I used to ask some of my biggest critics why they were out hunting, and many told me they were looking for "security" and "love." (Funny how the love came second.) But I was an independent woman who didn't want to share her life with someone all the time. I'd already done that, and I wasn't interested in doing it again. Again—you have to be really confident in yourself to **Bag 'n' Tag**. I give myself all the security and love I need. You should, too. (You should, regardless of your chosen hunting method. But you *must* if you're going to **Bag 'n' Tag**.)

The Art of the Bag 'n' Tag

In practice **Bag 'n' Tagging** is quite simple. You use the same methodology you would for **Trophy Hunting**—defining your **kill zones** and building your **deer stand** during the **Off Season,** and then allowing the **bucks** to come to you during the **Open Season.** Throw out **corn** in a non-threatening and non-obvious way. Find common interests with your **buck.**

The tricky part is that, as a **hunter,** you need to be able to keep your relationship simple and truthful, while also remaining classy. I just don't go up to some guy and say, "Hey, let's screw and be friends." You need to be a little tactical in how you lay the foundation of the noncommittal part of the relationship—and you also need to be a very good, very quick judge of character. Remember—you don't have as much time as **Trophy Hunters** have to determine a **buck's** worthiness. You need to get a good understanding of your prey in a matter of minutes. I usually give myself half an hour to make a decision when I'm **Bag 'n' Tagging.**

So, make good decisions quickly. I always begin by asking

my **buck** lots of open-ended questions, and paying close attention to his responses. Not only do I learn a lot about my
buck very quickly, but it also makes him feel important and
interesting. (Never underestimate the value of stroking a
buck's ego.) Learning how to do this without turning your
conversation into an interrogation takes some doing, but
practice makes perfect. During **Off Season** I practice this
technique on every **buck** I meet, whether I find him attractive and interesting or not. That gives me the opportunity to
perfect the skill with no vested interest in the outcome.

Once you've determined that you do want to **bag** the
buck you're talking to, then you have to move the conversation from talking about him to talking about bringing him
home. I like to give an indication of my intentions with a
quick comment or two referring to the next morning or the
expected fun to come (i.e., "How do you like your coffee
in the morning?" or "Before we go to my house, let's pick
up cigarettes or a bottle of wine." I try to stay away from
ambiguous flirting comments like "Let's see what happens
tonight," since the whole point of the **Bag 'n' Tag** is that you
can be quick and direct.). When you throw these comments
out, watch closely for his reaction. If he becomes distracted
and nervous, let him go. You're not trying to trick him into
becoming prey. He should want it as much as you do.

Setting up the proper groundwork, as I described in the previous two paragraphs, is really important, because with **Bag 'n' Tagging** the final moment of the kill isn't subtle at all. Remember: this method is about honesty and upfrontness. I simply say, "Okay, let's go home." If you've done good hunting work, the **buck** will say, "Okay," and then you'll leave together. Successful hunt! (Note: Even though you should only spend half an hour deciding whether you are going to bring your **buck** home, you should not extend the offer to go back to your place in that initial time frame. It takes an entire evening—several hours, at least—to properly set up the kill.)

But Elle!
I Fired and Missed!

In a perfect world we **hunters** would **bag** every **buck** we'd like to—well, the world isn't perfect, is it? When you finally fire at your **buck**, you should always be a little prepared for him to say no. That happens sometimes. The more you **Bag 'n' Tag**, the less this will happen to you, because you'll get better and better at reading signals. But even when you're an expert, some **bucks** send all the right messages and then choke at the last minute.

If your **buck** declines your proposition, don't take it personally. Smile graciously and release him back into the wild. Some **bucks** will ask for your number before they go. Go ahead and give it. (Again, you want to be gracious and classy. You're in your own **deer stand**, after all, and you want to be able to continue using it.) But I never go back to **bag** what I couldn't bring down the first time. Returning to a **failed capture** always makes me feel like I'm the prey instead of the **buck**, and usually comes about when the **buck** manipulates the situation so that he is more comfortable the next time he spots me in my **deer stand**. Steer clear of that.

I'm a pretty experienced **Bag 'n' Tagger**, and it's rare these days that I fail to bring down (or home) a **buck** who wanders into my **kill zone**. But **Bag 'n' Tagging** does take some practice. Trust me, you will have some mini-disasters. That is why having self-love, confidence and self-respect is really important for **Bag 'n' Taggers**. If you've had one of those days that makes you feel bad about yourself (and don't we all have them?), don't head out to **Bag 'n' Tag**. One bad **buck** can demoralize a **hunter**. Don't head out to the woods looking for a confidence boost. You need to head out fully confident and prepared.

Remember: **Bag 'n' Tagging** is not a series of one-night stands. Most of my **Tagged Bucks** have become friends. I care about how they're doing and they are kind and respectful toward me as well. We have a mutual love without being "in love." When I **tag** a **buck** who doesn't treat me that way, I get rid of him during my **Off Season** stable cleaning and bring in fresh meat the next time **Open Season** rolls around.

One-Night Stands

As I've mentioned many times, a one-night stand is not the same thing as **Bag 'n' Tagging.** One-night stands usually happen when a **hunter** is intoxicated or on a rampage. (How many women can fess up to a sober one-night stand? Not me, that's for sure.) Unlike **Bag 'n' Tagging,** one-night stands rarely have anything to do with enjoying a **buck's** company and time. Do not **bag** a **buck** you don't want to spend more time with. That is wasted energy, and it's not **Bag 'n' Tagging**; it's getting plucked and fucked. If you get a bad vibe from a **buck** while you're in **precapture**, release him back into the wild immediately. Don't waste precious **kill zones** and hunting time on a **buck** you don't want to see again.

The Stag

Let's talk about the **stag** for a moment. You know a **stag** when you see him: movie-star looks, cocky demeanor, oozing sexiness. **Stags** turn the heads of both men and women—and they know it. My personal advice is to beware and avoid the **stag**. But I know from long experience that many **hunters**—even good, experienced ones—cannot help themselves. They live for the thrill of throwing caution to the wind and carefully tracking this majestic **buck**.

So let's assume you're going to ignore my advice and hunt the **stag**. First of all, this type of **buck** is *only* for **Bag 'n' Tagging**. No **Trophy Hunter** has any business going after the **stag**. Even if you do manage to lure him to your **kill zone**, he will never stand to be **mounted**. Don't even try.

The second important piece of knowledge regarding a **stag** is that he thinks he is hunting you. The thrill of the chase is what he lives for. And that is actually excellent news for **Bag 'n' Taggers**. You know how karate masters tell their students to use their opponent's weight and strength against them? The same applies here. I use the **stag's** need to hunt against him, to aid me in bringing him down.

Side note: This is the one time I consider the **buck** an opponent, and that is because that's the way he sees it. Even though in the end we both want the same thing, we're competing to get it on our own terms. **Stag** hunting is a game that both **hunter** and prey agree to take part in. Who ends up the **hunter** and who ends up the prey depends on who plays the game better. Though I have only lost this type of competition twice in my life, both times I had a rough recovery. **Stags** can very easily derail even the most experienced **hunter**, and I advise all **Bag 'n' Taggers** to think twice before setting out to capture this type of **buck**.

An Elle Real-Life Example: Hunting the Stag

I once had a **stag** engaged in a very close hunting match. Though we cared for each other (see above: even **Bag 'n' Tagging stags** should not turn into one-night stands), I must admit that the hunt had started to become more intriguing than the actual kill. We were both more heavily invested in who would be the "victor" than in growing our relationship.

One morning I had left my **stag** at his Southampton, Long Island, house and returned to the city. That night I was introduced to another **buck** by a mutual friend. I knew that my **stag** would hear about this introduction, and that was okay by me. I didn't plan on **bagging** this other **buck**, but it was the **Open Season** and I never turn down an introduction during those months. Well, it couldn't have worked out better. When the mutual friend and I showed up at the restaurant where we were meeting my second **buck**, I glanced in the window from the street and guess who was sitting and talking to the new **buck** I was to be introduced to? Sure enough, **my stag** (who, by the way, had told me he would be staying in Southampton that evening. See what I mean about game playing?).

I played it cool and pretended not to see him—by the time I got inside, **stag** #1 had returned to his table, across the restaurant from where I was meeting **buck** #2. My **stag** watched me for over an hour. I surreptitiously kept my eye on him, and when it looked like he had had enough, I decided to put him out of his misery and went outside for a cigarette. Naturally, he followed, and in that moment I emerged the **hunter** and he, the prey.

Now here's an interesting twist in the story. A year after this experience, that **stag** came to me and asked if I would have a baby with him. He wanted to have children, he explained, but wasn't sure he wanted a typical wife. He told me that I knew and understood him better than anyone else, and he thought we would make a great couple as well as produce wonderful kids. I was dumbfounded and flattered, but I turned him down. Not only did I already have a wonderful son, and was not ready to raise another child, but I had **Bag 'n' Tagged** this **buck,** which meant that our relationship did not have the appropriate groundwork for commitment and child rearing.

I'll say it one more time: do not pretend you want to **Bag 'n' Tag** if what you're looking for is a **Trophy**. If you want a

buck to screw to your **wall**, you will never be happy with a **stag** or any **buck** you've **Bag 'n' Tagged.** The ground rules for the relationship are too different. It is true that **Bag 'n' Tagged bucks** do sometimes start to feel the need to capture their **hunters,** especially if she is a true **Bag 'n' Tagger** (very aloof with many a **tagged buck** to keep her company— **bucks** sometimes can't resist the thrill of the chase). But you cannot violate the rules of **hunting** and expect to come out unscathed. My **stag**, as you'll note, did not want a "typical wife." If you want to be a typical wife, do not **Bag 'n' Tag**. You should be **Trophy Hunting.**

Bag 'n' Tagging: Knowing When To Be Firm

Knowing when to send your **tagged buck** away is key to keeping him sniffing around. The **Bag 'n' Tag** relationship is not the same as a **Trophy Hunted** relationship. You are not required to—nor should you—spend an excessive amount of time with your **tagged bucks.** It's an unfortunate truth that when you have become an experienced **Bag 'n' Tagger,** your **tagged bucks** may want to linger—spend the weekend with you, for example, when you've only asked him for an evening. Do not let him stay. If you give him the wrong impression, you run the very real chance of souring the **bag,** and wasting all the hard work you've put in setting the **buck** up for future **tagging.**

Proper preparation for **Bag 'n' Tagging** is exactly the same (and as important) as it is for **Trophy Hunting:** don't **seasonally** or **geographically poach** (see Chapter 7 for more about that); spend your **Off Season** scouting and preparing your **kill zones,** etc. But when we're looking to **Bag 'n' Tag,** we can have a little more fun with placement of **deer stands** and appropriate **kill zones.**

Location, Location, Locations . . .
Ripe for a Bag 'n' Tag

When you're looking to **Bag 'n' Tag,** a vacation or an event can be a **deer stand** in and of itself. I mentioned above that I liked to take vacations with my **tagged bucks,** but what I didn't say was that if I don't happen to have a **tagged buck** on hand when I want to take a trip, vacationing is a great place to **bag** a new one. Puerto Rico, for example: that entire island is one big **kill zone** for me. I was there for four days on my own a few years back and can't even begin to describe how plentiful the game was.

But my favorite **Bag 'n' Tag kill zone**, bar none, is Fleet Week. For those **hunters** who do not live in the New York metropolitan area, Fleet Week is when the U.S. Navy and Marine Corps dock their ships, loaded to the gills with uniformed young **bucks,** for an entire week in New York Harbor. And all the young **bucks** have a week of furlough, conveniently coinciding with Memorial Day (smack in the middle of **Open Season**). Though I usually tell **hunters** to look for

quality over quantity, I do make an exception for Fleet Week
(for the **Bag 'n' Taggers** only, of course). I also recommend
that inexperienced or first-time **hunters** come to town for
Fleet Week. Just seeing all the beautiful **bucks** roaming
around is inspiring, and can give your season a real boost
(sometimes after the flush of the first few April weeks, the
Open Season can slow down to a more steady rhythm). And
Fleet Week is such a natural **kill zone**—with **bucks** actively
looking and hoping to be hunted—that you don't need to
do much set-up work if you're an out-of-towner (though if
you are an experienced **hunter** and a native New Yorker, you
should do a little groundwork prior to the week—scout out
some favorite restaurants and bars to take **bucks** to during
the precapture, etc. This ensures a good capture during fleet
week).

Other "natural" **kill zones**—places that don't require much
advance work and are ripe for **Bag 'n' Tagging**—include ski
resorts, surfing hot spots, and anywhere many **bucks** flock to
take part in a physical activity. I also happen to love having
international **kill zones**. I have cultivated **zones** on the north-
ern shores of Sweden and the hot beaches of the Dominican
Republic, with many stops in between.

Always be on the lookout—even during the **Off Season**—
for places and events that would be good for potential **Bag**

'n' Tagging. I recently took up cycling again. My biggest fear was having to change my own tire during a 100-mile ride that I signed up for. I was pretty afraid I wouldn't be able to do it. But while training for this ride, I happened to blow a tire. I cannot tell you how many **bucks** came to my rescue, all of them sweaty and in tight cycling shorts. Now, during **Open Season**, I sometimes go out and pop my tires and wait for them to come.

Bag 'n' Tagging: To Sum Up

I hope I've given you a good introduction to my world of **Bag 'n' Tagging**. I could not be happier here, and I hope some of you will decide to try it for a season (or more). Trust me, you won't be sorry . . . and should you return to **Trophy Hunting** after just a season or two—well, you'll still have memories to last a lifetime.

Chapter 6

Off Season

_____

Where there is a beginning, there must be an end: **Open Season** naturally leads into the **Off Season**.

The **Off Season** runs from September 30 through March 30. **Off Season** serves three very important masters. It prepares us for the upcoming **Open Season**—setting up our **kill stands** and gathering our **corn** (see Chapter 1, **Open Season**, for more there). It allows us to lick our wounds and reenergize after an **Open Season** that hasn't brought us the **buck** we've been hunting. And, third, **Off Season** is when, if we've had a successful **Open Season**, we see how our **buck** responds to captivity. I cannot say it often enough: you cannot have a successful **Open Season** without a productive Off Season.

In Chapter 1, **Open Season**, I explain why the **Open Season** months are perfect for hunting. The **Off Season** months are timely as well, and not just because they are left over from **Open Season**. Let's take a look at what events fall within **Off Season**: Thanksgiving, the Jewish high holy days, Christmas, Kwanzaa, Chanukah, New Year's Day, Super Bowl Sunday, the big V (Valentine's Day) and St. Patrick's Day. All these days are **Tension Days**—holidays and events in which family gets together and/or love tokens are exchanged. Expectations of our love interests run high during these days. In Chapter 1 I discuss in detail the dangers of hunting during this time, so I won't rehash it here. In this chapter I want to discuss what a **hunter** does when not hunting and how we use this time to our advantage.

Have you ever done anything 24/7, 365 days a year, with no break? The only thing I've done that often and regularly is breathing. Yet when I tell women they cannot hunt 24/7, 365, they are bewildered. I've got two words for them (and

you): *effective* and *exhausting*. To do something well, reju-
venation is required. The body and mind cannot focus on
one thing forever without eventually cracking. We need vacations from work. We need to eat out instead of cooking
at home every once in a while (and vice versa). Even pro-
fessional athletes take time off from training. It's the same
with hunting. If you do not take a break, you will end up
roadkill—limp and beaten (figuratively).

Off Season is when **hunters** are able to step back and take
a serious look at the most recent **Open Season**. Were you
satisfied? Evaluate your **kill zones** and **herd cultivation** techniques. Were you happy with the **bucks** you found in your
line of sight? Did you successfully bring down the **bucks** you
aimed at?

Beyond your basic hunting goals, successes and failures,
what did you learn about yourself? If you were a **Bag 'n'
Tagger**, do you think you might want to **Trophy Hunt** next
Open Season, or vice versa? If you think you want to change
your **hunting strategy**, ask yourself why. Are you giving up
on finding a **Trophy**? Has your life changed somehow, leaving you not ready for commitment? Or are you finally now
ready for that commitment, tired of the constant stream of
Bag 'n' Tagged bucks? There is no wrong answer to these
questions, as long as you give them some real thought and

understand your reasoning. **Off Season** is a great time to get honest with yourself as a **hunter**, a woman and a person. It's a time to fall in love with you again. Women who don't take an **Off Season**, who just hunt and hunt and hunt, are in danger of never taking the time to ask themselves who they are and what they are looking for. Eventually that shows up in a negative way in their relationships, whether they be of the **Bag 'n' Tag** or **Trophy** variety.

Not only does the **Off Season** provide a time to review our goals and motives, but it also gives us time to do some fixing up. This is the time to find and develop your **kill zones**, **cultivate your herd**, brush up on your hunting skills and do an all-around maintenance check. If you had a bad experience hunting—or, worse, ended up as **roadkill**—use the **Off Season** to evaluate what went wrong, go over your skills and techniques, and see what needs tweaking. Reflection is important; it can resolve hidden feelings that compromise your hunting. But we don't want to disrupt our hunting with overanalysis or questioning our behavior. During **Open Season**, put your doubts and concerns aside, to be examined and evaluated during the **Off Season.** Compartmentalizing like this takes some practice at first. But keep working at it and soon it will become second nature.

Personal Housekeeping

Off Season is a great time to take advantage of certain physical or lifestyle goals you may have. I personally do not put a whole lot of weight on "weight." As a **hunter** you have to be comfortable in your own skin, and we have seen plenty of examples from Hollywood of starlets who weigh all of three pounds and yet still have serious self-esteem and respect issues. But maybe you want to tone your arms a little, or grow your hair longer. You've got six months in which you will be focusing more on yourself than on potential **bucks**— now's the time to make those changes you've been wanting to make for a while.

This **Off Season** housekeeping also extends to any emotional wreckage you've got lying around. I had a good friend—let's call her Happy Hunter—who was a great **Bag 'n' Tagger**. She was able to bring down nearly any **buck** she positioned in her sights and she would set him free the next morning with no regrets. But all the nights out and socializing had started to affect her negatively. Happy Hunter started to break some of the **Seven Deadly Sins of Hunting** (see Chapter 9). The one that concerned me the most was her regular hunting under the excessive influence of alcohol. During the **Off Season** she joined up with AA, did what she needed to do, and was ready and sober to continue to **Bag 'n' Tag** when **Open Season** came around again. But a funny thing happened: after taking care of her personal housekeeping she realized her method of hunting needed to change. She was now ready to **Trophy Hunt.** I am happy to report that Happy Hunter is doing quite well. Nothing's hanging from her **wall** yet, but her brackets are firmly mounted and are ready for a suitable **Trophy**.

Taking Bucks Through the Off Season

Off Season is also an important trial period for your newly hunted **bucks**. This is critical for the **Trophy Hunter**. (**Bag 'n' Taggers** use the **Off Season** mostly for reshaping their

kill zones and thinning out the **herd**.) But let's say you're a **Trophy Hunter**. You had a good **Open Season** and think you've bagged a **Trophy**. **Off Season** now gives you a chance to see if that **buck** is in fact worthy of being **mounted** on your **wall**. While I want you to avoid **Tension Days** during the **Open Season**, the **Off Season** is when you should embrace them. Seeing how your **buck** reacts to your life—and you to his—during these days will tell you a lot about whether or not he is a keeper. And you don't have to decide immediately, after one difficult Thanksgiving. The **Off Season** gives you six months to decide if you are going to hang up your gun the next **Open Season** in order to continue with this **buck** or if you're going to release him back into the wild come April 1. And if you know things aren't going well—say you've had three tough **Tension Days**—you don't have to wait for **Open Season** to release that **buck**. Spending some time solo before the **Open Season** begins allows you time to recover and heal. You want to be able to set out with a newly polished rifle and a spring in your step when **Open Season** begins again.

Let's go through the entire process step by step. You found a great **buck** during **Open Season** and have been having lots of fun. When **Open Season** ends you decide you want to keep seeing this **buck** and only this **buck**, so you decide to stop seeing your other **bucks** to date this one exclusively.

(Note: if you become intimate with a **buck** when you are **Trophy Hunting** I strongly suggest moving to exclusive dating, even during the **Open Season**. **Trophy Hunters** are not looking for multiple kills. Once you have truly decided on one **buck**, release your other potentials back into the wild. Not only is keeping them in your stable unfair to the **bucks**, but it isn't nice to other **hunters** who are looking to add to their **herds**.) Up pops the first of the **Tension Days**—Thanksgiving. Thanksgiving is the perfect first road test for a **buck** you think might be a keeper for two reasons: a) it's a natural time to introduce him to your family and way of life away from the urban forest, but b) you don't have the pressure of gift giving and **love tokens**.

A Note of Warning— Do Not Bring a **Buck** You Don't Really Like Through the **Off Season**

Keep in mind that these family introductions should only happen if you really believe this **buck** is a keeper. Doing all that work and building up that expectation if you know you don't want to nail that **buck** to your **wall** is more akin to sending him to the slaughterhouse than releasing him back to the wild. I have a cousin who would always do the introductions, even if she knew her **buck** wasn't for her **wall**. Every **buck** she met would go through the same cycle—Thanksgiving, the holidays, New Year's, etc. It was an inside family joke that when her **buck** got to the final intro—to her father, who happened to live abroad—that would be the end of the line for him. We liked a lot of her **bucks** and we'd often be a bit sad when she announced the trip, knowing we wouldn't see that **buck** again. For years this went on and on, just like clockwork. But I am happy to say that that **hunter** has recently changed her poisonous routine and started being more discriminating about which **bucks** she chooses to bring through the **Off Season**. And—*bingo!*—she is happily involved in a great relationship that promises to go the distance. Good hunting skills at work!

So your **buck** makes the cut for the **Off Season** introductions. Great! If you haven't been intimate with your **buck** (see Chapter 4 to see how long you should wait), and the first **Tension Day** is approaching, wait to see how that pans out before making the decision to take the relationship to that level. The first **Tension Day** (Thanksgiving) goes well. Keep doing what you've been doing, enjoying your **buck** and seeing how he fits into your life.

The next **Tension Days** of Christmas, Chanukah and New Year's can be real tough ones. Right around this time, women love to start crafting a story about where the relationship is going. You know what I mean—you start imagining how his mother will love the gift you bring her, where you'll spend New Year's together, all that stuff. BE VERY CAREFUL to keep your actual behavior real and grounded. And please, please, please refrain from overly high expectations. Until you have had a natural conversation regarding the next level of commitment, you cannot expect that simply because the season of giving is approaching, the "gift" of commitment will just pop up. This is real life; we do not live in Lifetime movie specials.

Take a moment and think of all the friends you have watched break up after this time of year. How many of those were caused by unsatisfied expectations that escalated into arguments and unforgivable actions? I can't say it often enough: do not push the envelope during this time. Let the natural progression of the relationship take its course.

Tension Days and Gift Giving

Ideally, even though the holidays are called **Tension Days**, you will take as much tension out of them as you can. A good way to keep things grounded and easy is to discuss gift giving and holiday plans prior to the holidays. Setting boundaries and guidelines for gifts and attendance at various family events really helps prevent misunderstandings and hurt feelings. And though discussing the parameters of gift giving in advance may not sound very romantic, neither does a breakup.

Think of it this way: by discussing these subjects you are educating your **buck** for the future. If the relationship continues to work and you end up nailing him to your **wall,** he will already know for the coming years what you like and expect (you will let him know gradually as your parameters change). Basically, you're allowing for future romantic surprises that are happy events.

When I was a younger and more arrogant **hunter,** I used to have a laminated "gift sheet" I provided to all my **bucks**

(**Trophy** or **Bag 'n' Tag**). This sheet listed my ring size, shoe size, bra size, favorite perfume, and favorite flowers. I even gave actual gift suggestions for those **bucks** with no imagination, and, most critical, I listed forbidden gifts that would never be acceptable. I *do not* suggest that modern **hunters** do exactly this (certainly don't laminate!). But I would suggest doing a softer version of this cheat sheet if you are in a solid relationship with your **buck**. Don't be offensive or selfish when offering this helpful tip sheet to your **buck**; don't make unrealistic demands (i.e., a ring) or list gifts he's already given you as unacceptable. The purpose of such a list is to set some guidelines, not put down in writing your dreams and desires. In fact, if both of you make a gift sheet for each other, then this list becomes a mutually responsible action. **Bucks** love knowing that you won't buy them a tie when what they want is the hottest new Xbox game. You've made it easy for them to shop for you; and there are no hurt feelings.

As Open Season Approaches Again

As **Off Season** progresses into the later winter months, the **hunter** should be looking at the evolving relationship with the **buck** of her choice and asking herself if he is all she thought him to be. Does your **buck** possess the qualities on your list (remember, the one you made prior to hunting him down? See Chapter 2 if you don't know what I'm talking about). If he doesn't (or even if he does), are you happy with him? Does he fit into your life? Before the new **Open Season** rolls around, you need to decide whether you're going to keep him or dump him. Do not dismiss any issues as "small" or "not important." If you are having a problem with something, it is an important issue.

Here's another concept I can't highlight enough: you are not hunting for a **buck** you can "fix." If something doesn't feel right, that's a warning sign. No **buck** is perfect, and there will be things about your chosen **Off Season buck** that make you crazy from time to time. But you need to decide that those things that make you crazy are also things that you are happy to live with. You will never, ever be able to change a

buck's stripes (yes, I know, that's a mixed metaphor), and as a **hunter** you want to make sure that you do not give up an **Open Season** just because you weren't honest with yourself and stayed with what you knew would be a **failed capture**. Every day only comes around once. Don't spend yours with someone you have talked yourself into loving. It is far, far better to let a **buck** go, spend the rest of the **Off Season** dealing with the pain of it, and then recoup and **gear up** for the next **Open Season**.

Off Season: The Bag 'n' Tag Version

Now, for my **Bag 'n' Taggers, Off Season** is a time to perfect your hunting skills, get your **kill zones** set up, and clean, repair, and restock your **gear**. Just because you do not have a **Trophy** to check out doesn't mean you have to spend the next six months alone. True, you aren't allowed to hunt. But that doesn't mean you cannot recall those **bucks** you previously **bagged**. **Off Season** is the time to call in the **tag**.

When some women hear about my method of **Bag 'n' Tagging**, they tell me, "I don't do one-night stands." Well, neither do I. True one-night stands are a waste of energy (see Chapter 5 for more on the difference between one-night stands and **Bag 'n' Tagging**). **Bag 'n' Tagging** allows me to have companionship without commitment, companionship that can be recalled again and again through the long, cold winter months (assuming you do not live down South, in which case it's the long, dark nights). Imagine, New Year's Eve, holiday parties, Superbowl Sunday and even Valentine's Day, all covered with one quick phone call. I have even taken great vacations with my **Bag 'n' Tagged bucks**. I called the **buck** who skis and went to Utah for a week, then called another **buck** to accompany me to Puerto Rico for a different week. We had great conversation and even better sex—plenty of comfort, and no surprises.

While I love the thrill of the **bag**, my favorite part of **Bag 'n' Tagging** is what I get from **tagging**. **Tagging** allows the **hunter** to have a mini-relationship without all the pressures and commitments of a **Trophy**. A good stock of **tagged bucks** is what gets me through the **Off Season** as I plan for the upcoming **Open Season**.

Just like **Trophy Hunters**, **Bag 'n' Taggers** should also use the **Off Season** to weed out **bucks** that were incorrectly **bagged**. Even the most experienced **hunters** do not always have perfect instincts. The **Bag 'n' Tagger** should spend the **Off Season** asking herself, just like the **Trophy Hunter**, how much she likes each of her **tagged bucks**, and whether they're giving her everything she needs and wants. If the answer is no, dump that **buck** back into the urban forest. This not only keeps you happy and healthy, but it also keeps your "stable" fresh with stock, if you get my hint.

Real-Life Example: **Seasonal Poaching**

I am closing this chapter with a stern warning for my fellow **hunters**. **Open Season** begins on April 1 and closes on September 30. The **Off Season** begins on October 1 and closes on March 31. You must not fudge those dates for any reason. I point in example to a good friend of mine. Let's call her Lexy. Lexy is an exceptional **hunter**. She is a fast learner and works her skills wonderfully—except for one thing. Lexy is always trying to extend the season one way or another. Last year on March 25 I got a call from Lexy that went something like this: "Elle, I met this great **buck.** He's so fantastic and I know I was only going to **Bag 'n' Tag** this season, but now I think I want this new **buck** to be a **Trophy.** And he just asked me out. What should I do?"

Well, I told Lexy that since we were still in the **Off Season,** she could change her method of hunting from **Bag 'n' Tagging** to **Trophy Hunting,** as long as she was willing to do some fast prep work on her **kill zones** and **gear.** But I also told her that since the season opener was in six days, she could not accept this **buck's** invitation to dinner until then.

Lexy didn't like that at all. She claimed that she spent so much time focused on her career that she deserved an extended **Open Season,** to make up for the official **Open Season** days she wasn't able to hunt. She ignored my advice, and you know how she ended up? **Roadkill.** Worst of all, by the time she limped away, **Open Season** was in full swing and she was too upset over this **buck** to enjoy it. I hate to say, "I told you so," but in this case I really rubbed it in. Lexy knew better. What I would have liked her to do was say to this potential **trophy buck**, "Hey, dinner sounds great but can you call me in a week?" (And if she had really wanted to have some fun with it, she could have ended that sentence with ". . . That's when the season opens." Now, that will give any **buck** something to think about.) I'll say it one more time: **Open Season** is for hunting and **Off Season** is not. During the **Open Season** don't be afraid to multi-task and run yourself a little ragged;

six months of rest is coming whether you like it or not. But don't mess with the natural circle of life if you want to avoid being **roadkill**.

One final note: Please, *for both my sake and yours, don't give your **buck** this book*. Though I am very serious about maintaining order in the seasons, I like to keep hunting a fun thing. If the subject comes up with your **buck**, keep the mood fun, frivolous and flirtatious, saying things like, "You know I cannot settle down with you till the moon and season are right." Do not say, "I can only hunt you down and capture you for my **wall** starting in April, because Elle says in her book that that's the way to **bag** a **Trophy**." That's psychotic, and no animal likes to hear that. Best of all is simply not to mention your strategy at all. **Bucks** do not understand our methods and we do not always understand theirs. Sometimes the less information we know about the other, the better.

Chapter 7

Poaching

oaching is the single biggest sin of hunting, and women want to do it all the time. I refer, of course, not to cooking your breakfast eggs, but rather, illegal hunting, both geographic and seasonal. In Chapter 6 we saw how "Lexy" refused to adhere to the proper **Open Season** dates, which left her maimed **roadkill** during prime, legal **Open Season** hunting. That was a great example of **seasonal poaching**, the lesser of the two **poaching** evils. In this chapter we will look at both **seasonal poaching** and the very damaging **geographical poaching**.

Seasonal Poaching

Seasonal poaching, as we saw with Lexy, is hunting new **bucks** during the **Off Season**. Just like every other **hunter**, I hate to pass up easy prey, especially a good **tree scratcher**, but, just like hunting deer (or any other kind of animal), **poaching** while hunting men is "illegal" for many reasons.

First of all, **seasonal poaching** depletes the **herd** and usually only brings in a weak **buck**. When you sight him wandering through the urban forest, you may think he's a great **buck**, strong and healthy, but the truth is that nature uses the **Off Season** to ripen **bucks** to their fullest. Trust me, the **bucks** you see during the **Off Season** are still immature and unready for your purposes, be they **Bag 'n' Tag** or **Trophy fare**. **Off Season bucks** are just looking for a place to rut, temporarily. **Hunters** who take part in this usually end up **roadkill**. Trust me: I have seen it time and time again.

Second, bagging a **buck** during the **Off Season** usually means the **hunter** has to clean and dress her kill right in the middle of all the **Tension Days**. For **Trophy Hunters** these are especially dangerous waters. You haven't spent any time with this **buck** to judge whether he is worth introductions on **Tension Days**. You might not even be sure if this **buck** will be around for the important **Tension Days**— but, regardless, most likely, expectations are building. This all has great potential to lead up to a pressure-filled, rushed dressing and cleaning to prepare the **buck** appropriately for those introductions, which the **buck** usually isn't ready for. You know where this ends up: the relationship with the **buck** collapses, leaving the hunter depressed, angry and upset, but, worst of all, distracted from the job she must do during **Off Season**: **zone** and **herd cultivation**.

An Elle Real-Life Example: Seasonal Poaching

Back in the day, I found a **buck** I thought was worth **poaching** for, so, disregarding the seasonal rules, I brought him down. At first it was wonderful. I enjoyed many lazy days and hot nights with this **buck**. Then the **Tension Days** of Christmas and New Year's came around. Well, he had made plans to take a ski vacation with friends and family before he had met me, and our relationship was so new that I had not yet met any of them. Given that, it didn't seem to make sense for me to accompany him, nor was there any way he would cancel his plans to spend the holidays with me, my friends and my family. He just didn't know me well enough yet, he explained. And even though I understood, and wasn't going to push the subject, to be honest, I was bummed.

Well after New Year's the Super Bowl rolled around. Back in October, long before I had met this **buck**, I had bought tickets to the annual Super Bowl event held at my cigar club, Club Macanudo. This was for members and their guests only. I look forward to it every year with great anticipation and wouldn't miss it for the world. By the time this **buck** asked about my plans for Super Bowl Sunday (remember, our relationship was still relatively new, so I couldn't assume he'd be attending important events with me), there was no way I could get another ticket. So we went our separate ways then, too.

You get the idea. Even though this **buck** and I liked each other well enough and enjoyed spending time together, we continued to operate as we had during the holidays—making plans separately more often than together. I lost a perfectly good **buck** to the circumstance of **Tension Days**.

I didn't come out of my funk until two weeks before **Open Season** began. And guess what? My **zones** weren't prepped and my **herd** was scattered. It was a mess. I didn't get things up and running properly till June. What a waste of time.

Much **seasonal poaching** occurs because single **hunters** start to feel lonely and envy those **hunters** who do have a (properly-caught-during-the-**Open-Season**) buck. Those feelings are normal, but you cannot let yourself be distracted by that. Do not compare yourself or your catch to what your **posse** has. That kind of thinking gets you nowhere but depressed and in trouble. Trouble like **seasonal poaching**.

Instead of allowing yourself to wallow in bad feelings

during the **Off Season** should you have no **buck** to share it with, turn that loneliness into usefulness. Go out with your posse to scout out new **kill zones** and cultivate new **herd members**. You may also want to take a good look at what your feelings really mean. Are you judging yourself by your relationship status? That's ridiculous. The most fabulous **hunters** don't spend the **Off Season** feeling sorry for themselves; they enjoy the time they have to devote solely to their wants and needs.

Bag 'n' Taggers are some of the worst **seasonal poaching** offenders. They claim that because they aren't looking for anything serious, they don't have anything to lose by bad **Tension Day** timing. Wrong! If you are a **Bag 'n' Tagger,** you have no excuse for seasonal poaching. The **Off Season** is why you spent the **Open Season tagging**. Now you should spend some time with those **bucks**. Get to know them a bit better and weed out your stable. You should have spent **Open Season** carelessly filling your pen. **Off Season** is when you take a good look at your **captured herd** and thin it out so you can begin the next **Open Season** with only the prime grade-A **bucks** on your speed dial.

So, have I made my point clear enough? **Seasonal poaching** is self-indulgent and a waste of time. It's like binge eating: it's enjoyable in the moment, but ultimately gets you nothing but a feeling of regret the morning after. Don't do it.

Geographical Poaching

Geographical poaching speaks directly to Chapter 9's "Seven Deadly Sins of **Hunting**," specifically Sin #4: hunting a buck that has been **tagged** by another. I will never understand why some **hunters** do this. Not only does it undermine our **hunting** network, but it never yields a good catch. I mean, really: if he goes **hooves up** for you while he's rutting with another **hunter**, what makes you think he won't do the same thing to you? Your **corn** is not that special, believe me. How many songs have you heard about this or that no-good cheating asshole? And yet **hunters** continue to **geographically poach** while spewing every excuse and self-justification in the book. I'll tell you right now: there is no excuse or justification for **geographical poaching.** Not only is it wrong, ethically, but the consequences down the path just suck.

When I meet a **buck**, one of the first questions I ask him is: is he available? And by *available*, I mean "not married, engaged, dating, sleeping with or any other involvement that would give another woman a reason to get pissed off with me." If the **buck** answers no, then I'm cleared for hunting.

Don't Just Believe Your Buck—
Use Your Head

Bucks, of course, sometimes lie through their big, cornhusk-stripping teeth. If that's the case, I have nothing for sympathy for you, as you have made every effort to avoid **poaching**. But hunting a **buck** who has hidden his **tags** is not consequence free; it often leads down the same **roadkill** road as conscious **poaching.** To prevent that, I make sure that I look for warning signs of a lying **buck**. These include: excessive texting, refusing to take a (or multiple) phone call(s) after looking to see who's calling, calling my cell phone without leaving a message, delaying introducing me to his friends and business associates, dirty looks from his best friend's girlfriend (this usually indicates that she was told to keep her mouth shut—a disappointment to the **hunters** network) or just basic excessive nervousness in public places.

The number-one hint that a **buck** is allowing himself to be **poached**, though, is his never wanting to bring you back to his apartment. Often he'll use the excuse that your apartment is closer, cleaner or bigger. That is bullshit. If he is telling you those things, he has a wife or girlfriend at home. Put away your gun and immediately head to one of your other **kill zones**.

If you do get a chance to go to his pad, I don't advocate snooping, but I do think it's wise to keep a watchful eye out for certain indicators: pale or pastel towels, feminine toiletries, scented soaps or, my favorite, a razor left in the shower in full view, despite the electrical razor near the sink. I do not care what any guy tells you, he doesn't use both. **Bucks** are one-razor shaving animals, and that razor in the shower most likely belongs to another **hunter**. (Even if it's a men's razor. I know plenty of **hunters** who prefer a MACH3 to the Venus.) If you see anything that makes you suspicious, again: pick up your gun and head to greener pastures. There will always be another **buck.** There is only one of you, and you have your sanity and emotional happiness to protect.

Help, Elle!
I Accidentally **Poached**!

Even if you take every single precaution I list above, it is possible that you will be duped one day. It's happened to the best of us. If you find out that you have inadvertently **geographically poached** someone else's property, don't beat yourself up. Just get out. I also do not advise searching out the other **hunter** to tell her what a rogue your shared **buck** is. That's not your job. Not only will you hurt this other **hunter**, but there's a good chance that this wasn't the first time her **buck** has been willingly **poached**. She will look for someone to blame and guess who she'll find right in front of her? That's right: you. Trust me: there is no way you can avoid getting out of this situation without smelling like dead animal. So don't linger. Get out and get clean.

The same goes for trying to argue with your **buck** about this predicament. If you find out that he is enjoying another **hunter's corn** as well as yours, do not waste your breath discussing it. Just move on. Abandon the **zone** in which you found him. That's why you must always spend the **Off Season** building a number of solid **deer stands**.

As I said, even the best of us can find ourselves in this predicament. I will tell you about something I am not extremely proud of: I myself have unwittingly **poached**. A few years ago, about four months after my conversion to Orthodox Judaism, I logged on to an online dating website for religiously observant Jews. (This was on the advice of a girlfriend's teenage children.) On my very first day I found many a good Jewish **buck** to converse with. But one stood out from the rest of the **herd**. To protect his anonymity I will call him Buckstein.

Buckstein seemed to be a **ten-point buck**: good-looking, suave and possessed of a sexy voice, an edge of danger dripping from each syllable. He did not live in New York, so our relationship began by speaking often on the phone. When he traveled to New York for business purposes I met him face to face, and, fellow **hunters**, I must admit it: my knees went weak. Everything I uttered was jibberish. This **buck** had me at "shalom."

Time passed. Buckstein and I continued to see each other. I knew that Buckstein was looking to get married, and that was okay with me, since at that time I was **Trophy Hunting**. (I had decided before **Open Season** began that I was **Trophy Hunting**, of course. Buckstein did not make me change my method mid-season. As you know if you have read Chapter 1, that is not allowed.) Now, keep in mind that I was **hunt-**

ing as an Orthodox Jew. Technically, Buckstein and I should not have been having sex, or even doing any touching. But as the relationship progressed, we weren't always playing by the rules. First phone sex entered our relationship, and then finally, we decided we would meet abroad for a little overseas rutting (what happens overseas stays overseas).

I backed out of the overseas trip at the last minute. For some reason I was overcome with the feeling of fear (not something I'm used to). What if he was the one? I asked myself. This overseas trip felt a little more like a **Bag 'n' Tag** activity than a good **Trophy Hunting** strategy. (Plus, remember, we both held certain religious views that we would be disrespecting.) So I made a story up about a family emergency and we never went abroad.

Even though I was glad we hadn't taken the trip, I felt guilty about lying to Buckstein. I finally confessed to the lie and the reasons behind it. Much to my dismay, Buckstein ended our relationship. Hint Hint: lying for any reason is never good for any relationship, regardless of which method of hunting you are doing. It sets a bad precedent and once you've been caught in a lie, that trust can never be fully regained, as I learned here only too well.

Time passed. I missed Buckstein terribly. Then, one day, I called him. (I handled his money, so I used that as an excuse to ring him up. Now you'll note that I do not advise hunting at work. Back then I was a less experienced **hunter**, as you'll see from the many rules I broke with Buckstein.) Buckstein and I reconnected. I was so thrilled to be around him again that I forgot my earlier hesitations and flew to my home country of Switzerland to rendezvous with him. It was wonderful. We had great days touring the city in which I grew up, and the nights were everything I had hoped they would be: no inhibitions, no fear, just a healthy honesty in and out of bed. Or what I thought was a healthy honesty, anyway.

Remember, Buckstein and I had spoken of marriage. That had been the primary purpose of our dating. On the third day of our interlude, while lying in bed, Buckstein turned to me and said, "Elisheva [that's my Hebrew name], we need to talk."

I thought, "Okay, this is it. Now we will resume dating and discuss our potential marriage and of course my moving to his country." My head was already full of practical concerns: getting a visa, selling my apartment furniture, telling my family.

And then Buckstein told me that he had married someone else two months before—right when we had been planning our first rendezvous. On top of that, he had the nerve to say that even though he loved me, he didn't think he could ever trust me to be faithful to him, so he married a woman he was certain would be faithful. That's right: he had the nerve to tell me he didn't trust me to be faithful even while he was cheating on his newlywed wife with me.

Well, what's a **hunter** to do? I kicked him out of bed, wished him *mazel tov*, and smoked a much-needed cigarette. I felt pretty awful. But I was also relieved that I hadn't married Buckstein. If he had been willing to cheat on his wife of only two months, he'd be willing to cheat on anyone. Had I **mounted** Buckstein on my **wall**, as I'd hoped to, I would still be spackling and painting over the wallpaper damage.

Poaching: To Sum Up

As I have, hopefully, illustrated clearly, **poaching** can be very damaging to the **hunter**. It's real simple: once a cheater, always a cheater. **Bucks** rarely change their ways overnight, and the one instance in which I've seen it was due to a deeply spiritual experience. Please don't kid yourself: you can't provide that, no matter how great a **hunter** you are. Unless you met this **buck** during a near-death experience (and, no, I don't mean a great orgasm), a cheating **buck** will cheat on you just as easily as he cheated on the previous **hunter**.

Got it? No **poaching**. Don't move in on another **hunter's buck**, and don't **hunt** during the **Off Season**. Those paths only lead to heartbreak and distress.

Chapter 8

Hunting Gear

"Dressed to kill" is the saying and the goal—pun intended! In our world of hunting, we don't want to **gear up** in camouflage. Well, maybe a camo bikini for the right occasion, but the blending-in part is a total no-no. Whether we are in the middle of the **Open Season** or are staking out our **kill zones** during the **Off Season**, how we present ourselves is key.

Would you go on a job interview or to your best friend's

birthday party in any outfit? Of course not. You tailor your look depending on your objective. It's not any different when you're hunting. Most **hunters**, no matter how inexperienced, understand this. Where confusion arises, sometimes, is in understanding which outfit achieves which objective.

Many different things influence women's choice of dress: upbringing, personal style, musical influences, political influences, weather and, most prominent, the fashion world. All these are valid in guiding our selection of hunting **gear**. However, we need to make sure we are weighing these influences in appropriate amounts. When we pay too much attention to one influence and not enough to the others, we run the risk of looking like a **greenhorn Hunter**; that is, we stand out in a bad way.

Greenhorn Hunting Gear

One of my favorite instances of **greenhorn hunting gear** is from back in the seventies, when some fashion guru came up with "gauchos." For those too young to remember, gauchos were a pants-like apparatus that ballooned out by the knee, tapering in at the ankle. Yes, that's right, they were basically a sack covering your lower body. If you were slim, you didn't look it once you put them on, and if you were short and curvy or even had one extra pound on your rear, you looked like a healthy-bottomed pear. It was awful to see women, including myself, follow this stupid fashion trend. We all looked like weebles that could waddle. It's amazing anyone caught any **bucks**.

This horrific flashback brings me to the biggest faux pas of **hunting gear**. Just because it's in *Vogue* or on the runway doesn't mean it's a good look. The gaucho era was a clusterfuck that some fashion designer thought up while either high or drunk and passed it to the general public as a bad joke. Look who designs these "looks": do they wear this stuff? NO. When you see designers at their shows in New

York during Fashion Week, they are dressed in Armani, not in the outlandish creations that slink down the catwalk.

Don't Gear Up Like Everyone Else

When **hunters** follow the "in look" they often toss their common sense out the window. Two summers ago, it seemed every girl, woman and female baby was wearing these little slipper shoes with a gold round emblem. I saw so many on the street I thought there must have been a giveaway. To my amazement I found out that all these girls had paid an exorbitant amount of money for these shoes . . . so they would all look like one another. That's hysterical. No **buck** would have known which designer made those shoes; in fact, the **bucks** must have thought that the women wearing them were part of some female cult.

I do have a more serious point about dressing to the same trend as everyone else. On a sunny morning I saw a **hunter** sashaying down the street in New York. She was gorgeous, walked with confidence, looked all put together—really was doing everything a successful **hunter** does as she patrolled the field. I really complimented her in my mind. Then I turned the corner and there was her identical twin. The only difference between **hunter** #1 and **hunter** #2 was that one was blond and the other brunette.

Now if I had been a **buck,** I would have been giddy over the fact that I had two types of the same **corn** to choose between. But neither would have kept my attention for very long. That type of **corn** was obviously abundant and faceless. Abundant and faceless is not the image we want to project! Our **hunting gear** should reflect who we are as **hunters**— how we are different from the other **hunters**, what our own specific signature is.

Now don't get the wrong idea and wear something so out there that you look like you're from outer space. Just try to use some common sense when it comes to letting the latest fashion dictate your wardrobe. If you want to see what **gear** attracts the most **bucks**, don't pick up *Elle* or *Vogue*. Those magazines are written by women for women. Instead, pick up *Playboy*, GQ, or *Men's Health*. The ads and fashions in those magazines are targeting the same consumer you want in your sights: men.

This is such a simple idea, yet again and again I see women **gear up** for other women. I cannot say it strongly enough:

if you are out hunting **bucks**, do not dress to impress other women. Our **gear** is an important type of **corn**. It's a way to convey certain things about ourselves, and should be treated as an adornment (definition: trimming, enhancement, embellishment). **Gear** is not a remaking or covering of the true **hunter**. Get my drift?

Trust Your Weatherman: Gear Up Appropriately

Just as you should use common sense to determine which fashion trends work for you and which don't, you should also use common sense to decide how to dress on any given day. I cannot tell you how many **hunters** I see out in the **field** in completely inappropriate **gear**. The funniest is on those brisk winter days, when I see women mincing through the snow in high heels. Watching them carefully pick their way around puddles and piles of snow, sometimes I have to stop and laugh. But nothing is funnier than when those little heels are coupled with an extremely short skirt, fishnets and a jacket that ends at the waist. Ladies, I want you to know that this look in sub-zero weather has a nickname among the **bucks** out there: "Kitty Cooler." Yes, it's extremely demeaning, but it's also, unfortunately, true. What are we thinking? It's cold out! Put on some clothes. Revealing all your **corn niblets** up front, whether they be frozen or thawed, is not going to get you noticed by the type of **buck** you really want.

The same goes for the sausage effect. You know what this is: when you squeeze your size-eight body into a size-two casing. You may be proud that the number on your label is small, but trust me, you look like an explosion waiting to happen. And what do you think those **bucks** out there are saying about you? Please, please, please dress your size. You are a **hunter**, not pathetic prey. Take pride in the way you look, and remember, daring dress shouldn't translate into cheap and desperate.

In Chapter 2 I talked about the importance of body language when setting up a **kill zone**. Well, if the **gear** your body is wrapped up in takes away from your message, it's counteractive to your goals. If you have to constantly "fix" or "reposition" your attire, rethink wearing it. This would include shoes you are not capable of or comfortable walking in, shirts that ride up, bra straps that fall, itchy stockings (scratching is not sexy—I avoid stockings like the plague), or my favorite—panties that ride up and give you a wedgie (and not always the rear area, if you get my drift).

An Elle Original Tip

To avoid those uncomfortable wedgies I simply no longer wear panties. Seriously, what a pain in the ass. Not only does this alleviate panty lines, which I hate, but there are other benefits. For one, I can pee in under a minute flat and when I am bored and have nothing to hunt, sometimes I'll make a wager about this with the bartender to get a free drink. Also, I don't have the added expense for sexy undies as opposed to everyday undies; I only have my "monthly undies." And best of all, I never leave an accidental token behind after one of my **Bag 'n' Tags**. Men love to collect underwear. Well, I ain't got any, so they're out of luck.

There are two exceptions to my "No Panties" rule. First, as I alluded to above, during a certain time of the month you do need to wear them. I hope I don't need to explain why. Second, it's a big no-no to bare your bottom while wearing a skirt or short shorts. Having your **buck magnet** hang out in open air is not only not lady-like, but in certain instances can create embarrassing situations. The last thing you want is your **gear malfunction** recorded for posterity in some **buck's** memory or, worse, on his Facebook page. Let me just say, "Britney Spears, Lindsay Lohan, and Paris Hilton." Did you get a little shiver? Don't make that mistake. Going commando is only good if you're wearing pants or longer shorts. If you're wearing anything else, panty up.

Gear isn't limited to what you wear to work or out on the weekends. You may be hunting, for example, in a **kill zone** that is based on some type of activity. So make sure you have the right **gear** for that activity and try it out at home first to ensure that everything fits properly. You don't want to be surprised by a malfunction out in the **zone**. Your bathing suits should tie well and shouldn't slip around—you really don't want anything to just "pop" out. Bike shorts shouldn't cut your circulation off at the knee (been there, done that, don't recommend it). Sports bras shouldn't squeeze you into a "uniboob," and sporty tank tops shouldn't fall down, revealing your sports bra. Activity **gear** can be fun and extremely sexy, so take care to wear it right and use it to its full potential.

Holiday Gear

The **Off Season** is full of holidays during which **gear** is paid extra attention to—the entire month of December is usually devoted to a number of holiday parties, for example. And then there's Halloween, which is a great opportunity to have a lot of fun and get a little outside of your box. (Not literally.) Again, when dressing for Halloween, please use common sense. How cold is it? Will you be comfortable and able to move in your **kill zone** in your chosen outfit? Do you look like someone will throw you a $20 bill if you sit on his lap (not a desirable effect)? I strongly advise staying away from the "hooker/nurse," "hooker/cheerleader," "hooker/you-get-my-point." Look, I also advise avoiding full-body costumes like an Oscar Mayer weiner, or the back end of the horse (or even the front end, for that matter). This sounds obvious, but you have to be seen to be seen.

My personal favorite costume is an elaborate vampiress—sexy and mysterious without putting everything you've got on display. Going as a **hunter** is also a fab idea—just think of the fun you can have with a sexy little tailored camouflage number. I make it a habit to have two outfits ready for Halloween. That way I have a backup for emergency weather changes, plus if I go to several festivities during the week, I won't have to show up in the same thing twice.

Now, as I mentioned above, Halloween does fall during the **Off Season,** so you can't pick up any new **bucks** during this time. But it's a good way to get to know one of your recently acquired **bucks** a little better, and it's also fun to check out new potential **kill zones** and the **bucks** that browse there.

Other Special
Off Season Days

Other **Off Season** dates that require special attire include New Year's Eve, Super Bowl Sunday and Valentine's Day. You will be out and about during these **Tension Days** and can or should be **cultivating the herd** for the coming **Open Season**.

On New Year's I recommend going for some sparkle. Don't go demure if you are alone; keep your outfit bright and happy so you can shine like a beacon for the **bucks**.

For the Super Bowl, I love doing the sport motif. But that can be overdone, so I like to put a classy spin on things. How different will you look coming into the party in a smart pencil skirt and college prep type of shirt with the name of the team you're supporting on the upper shoulder area? I also love pigtails for Super Bowl Sunday or for just attending sporting events. It's so college girl. I wear pigtails with a skirt and cashmere sweater to many football games. You have no idea the reaction this gets.

On the big V-day, if you are not with a **buck**, don't stay home and duck. Get out that gorgeous red dress (screw the little black dress) and go out with a girlfriend, sibling, or your mother. Let those **bucks** see how comfortable you are in your own skin. Even if you think you're not dressing up for someone "special," I can promise you that you are. You're dressing for the most important person in the world—yourself.

Labeled Gear

I would like spend a few minutes discussing a somewhat controversial topic: **labeled gear**. I was recently having a conversation with a **buck** friend of mine. He started talking about how a mutual acquaintance of ours dresses, in almost exclusively designer **gear**. I felt bad because there was little I could do to defend her in this conversation. Before I knew it, three other **bucks** joined in to laugh about other **hunters** they knew who dressed the same way. One of the **bucks** said, "Those [hunters] wear so many labels they should be receiving marketing compensation from the designers!" And you know what? They were right. All those **hunters** had the same type of bag, shoes, jackets, even jewelry. Many of them were single. Then one **buck** made the most important comment of the conversation. (**Trophy Hunters** especially, listen up!) He said, "Man, I would never date or marry so-and-so. I would spend more money to outfit her than I do on my mortgage." Laughter and acknowledgment went around the table as all four **bucks** agreed.

In the movie *Legally Blonde*, Elle (Reese Witherspoon) says to her fellow law colleagues that men know black shoes from white shoes, not whether they're last year's Prada. She's right. There are some exceptions, but for the most part **bucks** haven't the slightest clue if what you're wearing is designer or not. If it looks good, they think it's good. (After all, they are simple creatures. Majestic and intelligent, but nonetheless simple in many respects.)

What **bucks** do know is whether a **hunter** is out to spend their hard-earned retirement money on clothes. I am not against high-quality attire at all, but in our culture there is a real overexaggeration of the importance given to designer labels. Some women say, "If I can afford it, I should buy it." That's fine. If you can, you should. But if you cannot, worry about your retirement fund before you spend your last $500 on shoes. (Remember when Carrie Bradshaw couldn't buy an apartment because she had too many pairs of Manolos? Don't let that be you.) The only people who will appreciate a $500 pair of shoes that you cannot afford is your **posse**. And if the only thing your **posse** admires you for is expensive shoes, you need a new **posse**.

I have also been told, "If you want to marry rich, you have to look the part." I can personally name plenty of instances in which a wealthy **buck** has not taken that route. In fact, many wealthy **bucks** prefer dating women who aren't openly after their bankrolls. As I mentioned in Chapter 2, I don't advise hunting the very wealthy, for a number of reasons. For the purposes of this chapter, I'll just leave it at one question: if you do end up with a well-off **buck** who is more interested in what you wear and how you look than in who you are, ask yourself—are you still the **hunter,** or did you end up **mounted** on his **wall**?

Gear: Final Thoughts

Before I wrap up this chapter, I want to offer a few other **gear** specifics:

— Fingernails. We call them nails, not talons. We are human **hunters**, not birds of prey. Two-inch nails adorned with full museum-quality paintings can get in the way of many hunting acts. Not to mention that it's not classy to complain that you broke a nail during lovemaking.

— Toes: Keep them clean and smooth. Fondling your **buck's** scrotum with sandpaper feet is a turnoff. (By the way, assuming your toes are clean, that's a great move for after sex play.) Clean feet are often an indication of clean everything else.

— Remember your age: as I write this book, I am forty-two years old. I wear some "fun" things, sure, but I do not try to pass myself off as a twenty-two-year-old. Nothing is more embarrassing than an older **hunter** wrapping her wealth of experience in **gear** that is appropriate for a **hunter** twenty years her junior (and we've all seen that, haven't we?). Dressing inappropriately young also does a great injustice to the older **hunter**. **Hunters** over thirty-five don't need to compete with the twenty-five-year-old pack. The youthful **hunter** has youth. The cougar has claws. I have years of experience about how to treat a **buck** right, how to soothe him, how to treat his ego sensitively— everything I've learned over the years. The youthful **hunter** has no wrinkles. Act your age and be proud of it.

For the Youthful
Hunter

You've probably heard that women don't reach their sexual peak until their late thirties. Well, I've been there, and I can tell you for sure that that's true. I see so many young **hunters** trying to act much older than they are, and trying to push their **bucks** into decisions they might not be ready for. Don't rush to have the older-**hunter** look, or live too fast. Enjoy your youth! I highly recommend doing some **Bag 'n' Tagging** research before you commit to **Trophy Hunting**.

Plastic surgery: yes, plastic surgery counts as **gear**. I've just got one thing to say about surgically enhancing yourself: all the Botox and face-lifts in the world won't cover up who and what you are in the morning when the most important person looks at you . . . in the mirror. Don't let yourself believe you'll be happier or a more successful **hunter** if you just have your nose done/a little bit of Botox/a little bit of lipo. It's not true.

Never go out into the woods unprepared! Here's a list of gear every dedicated hunter should have (or, in some cases, should not have):

- Clean panties that do not leave lines or ride up (or best bet: none at all.
  (see page 146 for more on this)

- Grooming kit and razor to maintain clean feet, ears, hands, teeth, and genital area

- Breath mints

- A bottle of champagne or an expensive single malt scotch, so you can offer a tagged buck a drink. Many hunters keep wine around for this occasion. I think champagne and/or scotch are much nicer, and more memorable.

- Cigar cutter, in case your buck smokes cigars. If he doesn't, he doesn't have to know you have one. If he does, you'll be the coolest hunter he's ever met.

- A big supply of clean soft white face towels (see page 76)

- *How to Give a Mind-Blowing BJ* by Lisa Sussman. Especially important for hunters who are a bit timid in the bedroom.

- If you have a kama sutra book—hide it! You do not want to be a science experiment. Nor do you want to be a locker-room story.

- Never carry a pen, and do not put phone numbers into your phone. It's the buck's job to track you down.

- If you are using a *nom de plume* while you hunt, get used to it during the Off Season. You don't want your buck to think you're partially deaf because you only respond to your name part of the time.

- Throw out your Hello Kitty dolls. Replace them with cushy pillows in your bedroom and living room.

- MOST IMPORTANT: Hunting Jackets. Yes, that is what you think it is: condoms. Always, always have them on hand.

Got all that? Suit up, ladies, and happy hunting.

Chapter 9

The Seven Deadly Sins of Hunting

To every rule there is an exception. That is so very true—except when it comes to hunting. When you're playing around with loaded guns and large-antlered beasts, making an exception to the rules can have dire consequences. There's a reason we always check the safety on our gun.

The rules that I list below came about through much trial, error and pain. I grew up a Catholic schoolgirl, so I have always looked at rules as made to be broken. I wore my demerits like badges of honor. But when you're hunting a man, breaking these seven rules more often leads to "badges of shame." And I know you want to avoid that.

Let's get right into it.

Rule 1: Never Hunt with a Posse

This is the granddaddy of all hunting rules. Unlike the true sport, in which you hunt with a partner for safety, when hunting men the exact opposite applies. Unless you are willing to share the kill or, even worse, lose the kill altogether, don't bring another mouth to the table to feed. As I pointed out in Chapter 1, I am convinced that *ménage à trois* started when women hunted with **posses**. You find a **buck**, you have a friend along, and next thing you know, it's a love fest.

The idea of hunting alone, or going out to engage in activities by yourself without the "comfort" of backup, is frightening to most inexperienced **hunters**. I cannot count the number of women who have looked at me like I have a third eye when I suggest going to the movies, dinner or a sports event alone. And I'll admit: it can be scary, walking into someplace where you don't know anyone. But this is why **Off Season** is so important. That is when you ease yourself into "being alone."

Since you're not hunting during **Off Season** you can scope out potential **kill zones** and **deer stands** with friends without jeopardizing anything. As you do this, little by little wander away from the security of your group. As **Off Season** progresses and you start to develop your **zones** and **stands**, you will find that they start to become comfort zones in their own right, where you know people there—other regulars, like you—but you aren't actually "with" them. And then, when the **Open Season** begins, available **bucks** will just see the unusual sight of a woman entering alone with confidence and a smile. Being able to be alone is incredibly sexy and attention getting. And the **bucks** don't need to know that you spent months working up to it.

When you hunt alone, you are also more approachable— and more able to approach available **bucks**. You are free to go up to anyone without having to worry about leaving a fellow **hunter** behind, and on the flip side, the **buck** is more likely to approach you. **Bucks** have a great fear of rejection— but if you reject him and no one is there to see it or laugh about it later, did it happen?

Bag 'n' Taggers especially—hunting alone should be your golden rule. We of all people do not want to share our kill with anyone for the time we have them. Because we **Bag 'n' Taggers** aren't looking for a long-term commitment, we have a smaller window in which to close the deal than do **Trophy Hunters**. Don't put unnecessary physical and visual obstacles in your way.

Rule 2: Never Look Bitchy— Always Smile Like Grace Kelly

If you look it, **bucks** will think you are it. Have you taken a gander at some **hunters'** expressions recently? I have, and, wow, so that's where the saying "if looks could kill" comes from. I see many **hunters** walking around and think, "Damn, who would want to approach that, or, worse, wake up with it?"

In Chapter 2 I talked about the importance of being aware of your expressions. I think it's key to know what your face looks like when you react in certain ways. But **hunters** are not robots, and we have bad days. There are times when even I walk around with a "bad face" on. That's okay. I don't want you to pretend you feel something you don't, or to "act" a certain way. When you're having a bad day, don't hunt. You shouldn't be hunting 24/7, 365 days a year, anyway. Not even the lions do that. So if you cannot keep a genuine smile on your face and twinkle in your eye, hang up your gun and take care of whatever is bothering you. Finding a **buck** to lean on is not the answer.

Rule 3: Never Drink to Excess

I can't help but point out a famous NFL player who was out with his **posse** when he shot his foot with his own gun. Aside from the fact that this tale is about a man, it nicely illustrates Rule #3. Getting toasted and stumbling around the urban forest looking for a **buck** is not only pitiful to watch, but it's also just a matter of time before that **hunter** wakes up with a hole in her foot. Or even worse. I try to not be too serious about most of hunting, but ladies, this is where I am deadly serious. You go out and drink until you can't see straight, you're taking the chance on a truckload of bad things happening to you: making a fool of yourself, waking up with a case of **hunter's remorse**, nonconsensual sex or even worse. If you want to be out so you can drink, go out with your **posse** and leave the rifle at home. If you want to hunt, do it sober and clean. Remember, you are someone's daughter or mother and/or soon-to-be wife. Act like it.

Let's talk for a minute about **hunter's remorse**. Raise your hand if you've ever woken up with a case. (My hand is up.) **Hunter's remorse** happens when you bring home a deer who does not even deserve the name **buck**. You've seen these men out, and I bet you've wondered who the hell would ever go home with someone like that. Well, if you're swimming in the alcohol river, guess who's going to bring him home? That's right: you.

I don't mean to lecture. We've all done something stupid and lived to regret it. But **Open Season** is a time to play seriously. Don't drink and hunt.

Rule 4: Never Hunt Another Hunter's Buck

You've heard of the fabled "Boys' Club," right? Well, let me introduce you to the "**Hunters'** Club." Don't screw over your fellow **hunter**.

I don't care what your **buck** mumbles to you at night. If he goes **hooves up** for you, he'll do it to you, the moment a better **hunter** comes along. Because here's the harsh truth: you are not the best **hunter** out there. You may be very, very, *very* good. But there will always be someone else who has a bigger gun, has a sturdier **stand,** has **tagged** more **bucks**, has nicer **gear** (or looks better in it), blah blah blah.

Hunting isn't about being the best for your **buck**, but being *your* best for you. If you practice **poaching**, I guarantee you you will be cheated on. **Bag 'n' Taggers** have to be especially cautious of this rule. The fact that we're not looking for a commitment doesn't give us the go-ahead to **poach**. Allowing a **buck** to use you to cheat is just that: being used! And then you're back to being **roadkill** again.

There is nothing wrong with asking early on, "Are you married, engaged or seeing anyone?" If the **buck** asks why you are inquiring, **Bag 'n' Taggers** should say, "I don't fuck cheaters." **Trophy Hunters** can explain, "I do not want to waste my time on someone else's property." An older friend of mine (older in age, new to my friendship) once said to me, "Don't give up your integrity and don't be afraid to test him. An honest and good man will never be embarrassed by what you ask." (Thank you, Denis!) I found that to be profound, true and rarely followed by my fellow **hunters**. Follow Denis's advice. Be smart about not cheating.

Rule 5: Don't Be Afraid to Give up a Great Buck Who Isn't Right for You

A really good **hunter** can bring down almost any **buck** she lines up in her sights. But that doesn't mean that every **buck** is right for you.

I had a great Southern **four-pointer** in my sights one night. I can still picture him: tall, broad, young (twenty-six) . . . perfect. I made my move, took him down and brought him back to my apartment. As we spoke I found out that he had given up a chance at pro ball to pursue a career in something else (I must confess I don't remember what). I found him so charming that, and I am being completely honest here, I told him that I couldn't "enjoy him" for the night because I thought he was too nice for the regular **Bag 'n' Tag**. He had all the markings of a **Trophy**. So we sat in my bed, watched football movies all night, and had a great time. Now he is married to someone else. From time to time I still think of the great time I could have had with him, and to be honest, I have wondered if I should have maintained a friendship until the next **Open Season,** when I could have switched methods and **Trophy Hunted** him down. But would that have made me really happy? I don't think so. I'm glad I opted to let the **buck** pass in favor of his friendship. (Darling, if you're reading this: who's got heart?)

You can love and respect a **buck** and not want him for either a **Trophy** or a **Bag 'n' Tag.** Just because you can bring a **buck** down doesn't mean you should. Remember, you don't want to hunt a number of **bucks** who know each other, or who spend a lot of time in the same **kill zones**. Every time you bring a **buck** down, you commit to sparing the rest of his **herd**.

It's okay to just be friends with a **buck**. Don't force yourself into a relationship you don't want just because a **buck** is really interested in your **corn.** Sometimes being friends with one **buck** will bring another, more **Tag-** or **Trophy-worthy buck** into your sights.

Rule 6: Never Settle for Just Any Buck

Listen, **bucks** aren't fish, but there are plenty out there for the catching. Stop looking at the statistics of female-to-male ratio. That's crap. In fact, it's probably a number some **buck** decided to put out there to make **hunters** feel more desperate.

If your **buck** is not the right one for you, you know it. But knowing it and admitting it, even just to yourself, are two entirely different things. I have a good friend who is married to the wrong **buck.** She is trying to work it out, for which I give her credit, but we all know that he is not for her.

No **hunter** can rely on her friends or family to tell her she's **bagged** a dud. One: no one wants to tell her friend, sister or cousin that she hates her boyfriend. Two: no one wants to hear that her boyfriend should have been no more than a bad case of **hunter's remorse**.

My advice runs all the way back to Chapter 2. Remember that list you made of your "must-haves"? Don't start to cross things off the list because the **buck** you have in your sights has a number of qualities on your second-tier list, or because it's been a long time since you **bagged** anything. Every relationship should start off on the right foot, pointed away from Mr. Wrong and toward Mr. Right.

Rule 7: Tease Wild Animals at Your Own Peril

"Stop teasing the cat," your mom would scold. Did you listen? No—you kept pulling Muffin's tail until you were bitten. At the age of six, a Band-Aid and a cookie made you feel better. At the age of twenty-six, thirty-six or forty-six the Band-Aid better be a whole lot bigger.

Bucks are wild animals. If you poke at them enough, they will respond in anger. Don't shoot a BB gun at a **buck.** Either you want him or you don't. If you do, and you don't go after him with your best weapons, you are wasting your time and energy. If you don't, and you let him think you do, you are opening yourself up for retaliation. You think **hunters** hold the patent on gossip? Not true. **Bucks** will spread rumors if you give them a reason. Don't use them for target practice. They'll know, and their egos are fragile. Handle them with care.

A Final Thank You

When I was twelve years old, my mother took me to a Tom Jones concert. Tom Jones was playing in Atlantic City, New Jersey, where my father worked for Resorts Casino and Hotel. Now, I had no idea who Tom Jones was. I was flat-chested, gawky, and I wore glasses. I barely knew what boys were.

But, as I watched Tom Jones strut around the stage in his signature tight satin pants, something changed. And when he sang, "What's New, Pussycat?" and twitched his hips, I thought: *I have to meet him.*

After the concert hundreds of women got in line to greet Mr. Jones. They carried flowers, candy and brassieres to offer him. Seeing all the competition, I turned around, discouraged. But my mother encouraged me to get in line. "You can just say hello," she said. "That's just as special."

I was the last person to reach the stage. The entire time I stood in that line I was thinking about what I could give Tom Jones that none of the gorgeous women in front of me could. When I finally reached him, I motioned for him to come close to me, and I whispered in his ear, "Mr. Jones, if you give me a kiss my father will give you a free dinner at his restaurant, Capricio, here in the casino." Tom Jones stopped the band and quieted the crowd. Then he repeated my offer for everyone to hear, and followed that by giving me my first real grown-up kiss.

Well. Everyone in the casino immediately rushed to Capricio in the hopes that they would be able to get a table near Tom Jones. The crowd became so unmanageable that security had to be called in and the restaurant had to be shut down for the evening. My father's bosses were furious with my father; my father was furious with me; my mother was furious with Tom Jones—but I was glowing.

As we walked away, a man called out to me, "Hey, little girl, if I kiss you will you give me a free dinner?" I tossed my hair and looked over my shoulder (as seductively as a twelve-year-old virgin can) and replied, "Sure, at McDonald's."

I think we can all agree that a hunter was born that night. Mr. Tom Jones, thank you.

Glossary

4-Pointer—Man ranging in age from twenty-six to thirty-five years old

6-Pointer—Man ranging in age from thirty-six to fifty years old

8-Pointer—Man ranging in age from fifty-one to sixty-five years old

10-Pointer—Man over age sixty-five

Bag—Successful **hunting**: securing a date, bringing a man home, etc. The exact definition of **bag** will change depending on your **hunting method**

Bag 'n' Tag—Commitment-free dating

Buck—A man

Corn—Tidbits **hunters** use to entice new **bucks**; examples include witty conversation, good looks, classy attire

Cyber hunting—**Hunting** online

Cyber stands—Online **deer stands**, i.e., your profile on dating websites

"Deer in the Headlights" syndrome—When **bucks** feel that **hunters** are pressuring them to behave a certain way; often results in panicked flight from **precapture**

Deer Stand (also, more casually, **stand**)—Specific location (bar stool, mid-pack in the ten-minute-mile running group, etc.) where a **hunter** can lie in wait for a **buck**

Dismounting—Removing a **buck** from your **wall** (and life)

Failed Capture—**Trophy Hunting** a **buck** you decide you don't want on your **wall** after all

Failed Mounting—When a **Trophy-Hunted buck** does not call back and we lose him to the wild

Gear Malfunction—Any instance in which your hunting gear lets you down: a broken heel, a popped tire, a lost bikini top, etc.

Gearing up—Preparing to **hunt**

Geographical Poaching—**Hunting** another woman's bagged buck or on another woman's territory

Greenhorn Hunter—an inexperienced **hunter**

Herd—the group of men you successfully **hunt**, or, more generally, a group of **bucks**

Herd Cultivation (or, more casually, **cultivation**, **cultivating**)—Maintaining the group of men you see through the **Off Season**, or, more generally, targeting a group of men you would like to **hunt**

Hooves up—When a **buck** is happy to be **captured**

Hunter—A woman

Hunter's Remorse—Wishing you hadn't **bagged** a certain **buck**

Hunting gear—The tools every hunter needs to be successful

Hunting goals—One of two; see **Bag 'n' Tag** and **Trophy Hunting**

Hunting grounds—All the possible places a woman can find men

Hunting method—One of two; see **Bag 'n' Tag** and **Trophy Hunting**

Kill Zones—Areas where a woman will go to hunt in **Open Season**

Labeled Gear—Designer clothes

Love Token—Any gift a man gives a woman

Method Jumping—Changing your hunting method mid-season. Not allowed!

Mounting—Successfully bringing a **Trophy-Hunted buck** onto your **wall** (and into your life)

No-hunt zone—A **kill zone** a woman has decided to take a break from

Off Season—October 1 to March 31, the time when women remove themselves from active hunting

Open Season—April 1 to September 30, the only acceptable time for women to hunt men

Poaching—Hunting during **Off Season**, hunting another woman's buck, or hunting in another woman's territory. Not allowed!

Posse—A woman's girlfriends

Precapture—Early days of dating

Roadkill—What happens to a woman when she doesn't hunt properly

Rutting—Having sex, screwing, fornicating (you get the idea)

Seasonal Poaching—Hunting during **Off Season**

Seven Deadly Sins of Hunting—See chapter 9

Stag—A man who is a player

Tagged Buck—A man you see regularly

Tension Days—Holidays that often cause tension in new relationships: Thanksgiving, Christmas, Chanukah, New Year's Eve, Super Bowl Sunday, Valentine's Day, St. Patrick's Day

Trophy Hunting—Dating with the goal of a committed relationship

Velvet-Tipped Buck—A man under the age of twenty-six

Wall—A woman's life; the place she wants to put the **buck** she's **Trophy Hunting**

ELLE works in hedge fund operations by day, and hunts by night

Elle